Guvnor Ge

How I Survived Childhood Hell,
Football Violence, 50,000 Dexies and
United's Red Army

Andrew Bennion
(with Simon Eddisbury)

Fort Publishing Ltd

First published in 2011 by Fort Publishing Ltd, Old Belmont House,
12 Robsland Avenue, Ayr, KA7 2RW

Printed by Bell and Bain Ltd, Glasgow

Typeset by 3btype.com

Graphic design by Mark Blackadder

Front-cover photograph by Sam Fairbrother

ISBN: 978-1-905769-230

'There is a diminution in almost all the kinds of larceny. The same is true of forgery and coining but in regard to offences against the person and offences against property accompanied with violence, there is a tendency to a distinct increase. . . . The pickpocket is dying out . . . the hooligan replaces him.'

The Times, 6 February 1899

'All Stood Together'

by Andrew Bennion

All stood together,
A hundred miles from home,
In someone's city centre,
Waiting for it to go,
See their lads,
Coming fast,
Confusion in the air,
Look around,
Same old faces,
Difference is the place,
With nods and winks and knowing grins,
No reasons to despair.

Outnumbered and surrounded,
Adrenaline kicking in,
The buzz, the rush,
As you turn the tide,
Side by side,
We all stood together.

A hundred miles from home
Through thick and thin,
Week out, week in,
Win, lose or draw,
We all stood together.

CONTENTS

PREFACE

My story is not an easy one to tell, far from it. I don't expect sympathy or want it, just for people to understand. Those who know me, and I mean really know me, will get it. Others will remain ignorant but I will have done my best to explain my situation. I hope that some may see sense and maybe choose a better path than the one that I went down.

To the people who think that hooligans are the brainless Neanderthals that the media make us out to be, I hope that my thoughts will give you an insight into the reality behind the myth. No doubt a lot of people will be surprised when they realise that I'm not thick, given that I didn't go to school. I may not have had a formal education but I've seen a lot of life and learnt my lessons the hard way.

This book is not about glorifying violence at football nor is it about saying whether it's right or wrong. It's about me and the way I saw it. The heyday of football violence was an era when drugs, fashion, crime, gangs and music all came together, for better or for worse. Every aspect of the culture was intricately intertwined, like the motorways that crisscross the country, connecting previously alien landscapes to the rest of society. It was more than just a bunch of football supporters fighting with one another. It was the Hacienda, it was ticket touting outside Ian Brown and Happy Mondays concerts, it was the journey to the match and it was the trading of war stories between those who had been in the thick of the action.

Hooligans are the modern-day mods and rockers, scorned and criticised by the national media. But to me, they are my friends, my family and my confidantes. You may point your fingers at us but ask yourself this.

What's worse, fighting at a match or killing thousands of people for a piece of oil-rich land?

Andrew Bennion
Oldham
March 2011

THE FIRM

Before I start my story, I would like to acknowledge everybody who has gone to the matches with us over the years. Although this book has got my name on the cover it is as much about them as it is about me. Your mates can make the difference between life and death when you lead the kind of existence that I do. Here's a quick rundown of a few of the characters who stood alongside me and helped to make my life that little bit more bearable when times got hard.

Frankie

One of the original Young Guvnors, back when we really were young. He's been there for me through thick and thin. His mam didn't like him going to the football but she was still supportive of him. When he got nicked in Scotland, she drove all the way to Barlinnie to pay his surety. She deserves a mention for that; she was a good woman. Frankie's just celebrated his fortieth birthday and he had a decent turn-out for it, showing what a popular lad he is.

Little Spinner

A double-game lad from Wythenshawe who was always there to support me. He was one of my best mates and he's an all-round good bloke. He was living in a foster home for a while back when he was still fairly young and none of the staff had any idea he was a hooligan. They couldn't imagine him being involved with anything like that because he came across as such a nice lad.

Chrissie

A hard lad from Clayton who didn't give a monkey's. He always had a strong moral compass and even though he was one of the toughest people I've ever met, he was never one to bully anyone.

KC

My former next-door neighbour, a smart kid who passed his eleven-plus, O-levels and A-levels. Sadly he's been in a mental institution for the last twenty years.

Daft Donald

His cousin was a Chelsea fan and Donald got invited to London to go to matches with him. He was still green around the ears at that stage. 'We're going to do these Millwall bastards, aren't we mate?' one of the other lads asked him. 'Yeah,' said Donald. 'Fuck those Millwall cunts.' It really wasn't his lucky day. The fella that asked him the question was one of Millwall's lads and, the next thing Donald knew, he had been smacked on the head with a hammer. He's never been the same since. He's proper funny though, without doubt the firm's biggest entertainer.

Anthony Rowan

Another lad who was there from day one. He was one of the firm's gamest members and one of the soundest lads you could meet.

Leo Garvey

He was a good lad but, unfortunately, he ended up getting involved with drugs. Saying that though, we've helped each other through some dark times and he's been clean for years. He's a true blue and I've known him since we were both members of a teenage gang known as Gorton the Business.

Larry and ET (the Cockney Blues)

Larry was originally an Arsenal fan and ET was originally a Tottenham fan. I bumped into them in London when I was a kid and as it turned out they had a soft spot for City. I invited them to Maine Road, introduced them to the firm and they started going to matches with us. They were both sound lads, quiet and unassuming, but, when it kicked off, they would back you to the death. They may have been from London but they were City through and through. Larry died of cancer last year, he was only in his thirties. Nobody knew it was coming until it was too late and we miss him dearly.

Farmer

We called him Farmer because he was from Oldham and it's a little bit backward round those parts. Over the years, his passion has changed from hooliganism to extreme sports and he's proper into his mountain biking nowadays. I suppose it was a natural progression in a way because he was never scared of getting hurt and he was always in the thick of the action.

Patty

Another Oldham lad, as game as they come and a really sound fella as well. He was one of the first to follow England abroad by going to Mexico in 1982 and he was big mates with the Chelsea Headhunters.

Prestwich Chris

He told proper funny stories and he was always the first on the dance floor whenever we went to a club. Unfortunately, he ended up getting beaten over the head with a wheel brace and he stopped going to matches after that. I wasn't there when he got attacked but, according to the rest of the firm, he was so badly injured that you could see his brain poking through the hole in his head. I am also told that he 'died' three times on the operating table. It's ironic because he was a proper honourable geezer and he'd always use his fists rather than carry a weapon.

Clanger

As well as being one of our top boys, he was one of the first to go shoplifting abroad. I can remember seeing him bowling around in Lacoste and Dublin trainers and wondering how the fuck he got his hands on gear like that. He may have unduly influenced me to go out thieving but that was the only way that I was ever likely to get the finer things in life. He was a bad influence on me but he was always game and also very intelligent. I was banged up with him for a time while I was on remand.

1

WHIPPING BOY

I had the unhappiest of childhoods.

I always got on with my dad; he was chilled out and easy going. It was Mam I had problems with. It seemed to me that she was always hitting me and that when she wasn't hitting me she was shouting at me. She would no doubt claim that her behaviour was perfectly normal, that she was just instilling discipline, doing what a mother has to do to raise a child properly. But it didn't feel that way to me.

I loved my mum but I hated her at the same time. I was always running away, and not just down the garden path. I was being picked up a mile away from my house at two years old. I know her relationship with my dad was falling apart and maybe that affected the way she treated me. But if that was the case then why was she so much nicer to my younger brother, Steven? He could never understand why I kept trying to get away. But I felt like the family scapegoat.

Some people might wonder why my dad didn't notice that I was so unhappy and do something about it. But he was oblivious to most of what was going on. He was a bus driver and worked mad shifts, so, by the time he got home, I was asleep. My dad eventually became so exasperated by the state of his marriage that he went to stay at my nana's house and left me on my own with Mam. I can't say I blamed him. I would have gone with him in a heartbeat.

I was five when I made my last attempt to run away. I ran to my nana's road and hid in a garden at the top of the street. There had been an explosion at the nearby paintworks and all of the houses were covered in a thick, brown layer of tar. I knew that Dad was on his way home from work and I thought that if I waited there for him then I'd be able to jump out and surprise him. I remember the feeling of excitement when his van came round the corner. I wanted to run down the road to meet him but I was worried that Mam might be with him. I watched him intently as he got out of the van and walked across to my nana's. Then, when I was 100 per cent sure that he was on his own, I scurried over and tapped on the door, still shitting myself in case she was hiding somewhere. The ten seconds it took for him to answer the door were the most nerve-wracking ten seconds of my life. I kept thinking that my mam was going to come round the corner, grab me and take me back home.

'Andrew.'

It was Dad. Thank fuck.

'What are you doing here?' he asked me, looking bewildered that I had managed to get there on my own. 'You're filthy. Come on in and I'll get Nana to run you a bath.'

My nana was one of the few people who realised how I felt.

'Let's get you cleaned up,' she told me, a look of deep concern etched across her wrinkled face.

I loved my nana and I didn't want to worry her but I wanted her to realise how unhappy I was. She could tell something wasn't right. She had a sad look in her eyes, as if she sensed that I was being mistreated and desperately wanted to do something about it.

While I was busily scrubbing the tar off my blackened skin, my nana was having a heart to heart with my dad in the next room.

'This has to stop. You can't have him running away like this.' It was the first time my situation had been openly discussed and it felt as if a great weight had been lifted from my shoulders. My problems were real. Someone else was picking up on them.

'He should come and live here. I'll make sure he's okay,' Nana went on.

By this stage I had my ear to the door. I didn't want to miss a single word.

'Okay ma. I need you to help me with him though. I can't do it on my own.'

I was over the moon. I was going to live with Nana, the person I trusted more than anyone else in the world. It was the happiest day of my life and I remember running back to the bath and thinking, 'It's all over. I'm going to have a proper childhood.'

Nana lived in a two-up, two-down terrace house on Carberry Road in Gorton. She had an outside toilet and a coal shed and she had to make a coal fire in the morning to heat the water up. It was nothing fancy but, as far as I was concerned, it was the best thing since sliced bread. I had birthday parties, I went to school with clean clothes on, I had football kits, toys, colouring book. You name it. The only thing I didn't have was my own bedroom: Nana had one room; Dad and I shared the other. It wasn't that bad; it meant I got to spend more time with him.

During my spare time, I'd while away the hours playing in the pitch-black coal shed, revelling in the fact that I was completely hidden from sight. Mam wouldn't have approved of that. I was free to be myself without having to worry about rubbing anyone up the wrong way. Whenever Nana won at bingo she would buy me a present, Lego and toy tanks and the likes. I felt loved, wanted. I was no longer a scapegoat; I was a valued member of the family.

Then came the bombshell.

'I'm divorcing your mother. She's going to try to get you back,' my dad announced.

Legally, I was still her child, despite how I felt. My stomach churned and the thought went through my mind that I had escaped from hell only for the devil to grab me by the ankles and drag me straight back down again.

'The court is recommending that you see a child psychiatrist. They want to see how living with her has affected you,' he went on.

It would have affected me a lot less if I knew there was no chance I'd get sent back to her.

The psychiatrist asked me a load of different questions to figure out if it was a good idea for me to go back to Mam's house. I told him the truth, nothing more, nothing less. He recommended to the court that Dad should get custody.

I couldn't figure out why she was so desperate for me to live with her. Did she want to deny me the right to a happy childhood?

Later that day, a social worker took me into a side room and sat me down.

'I want you to think carefully about how you answer this question,' she instructed me. She had a look of grave seriousness about her, as if I was about to make a decision that would determine how I was to spend the rest of my childhood. 'Whatever you say now will happen. I want you to remember that.'

I wasn't used to having a say. Normally, whatever my mam said went.

'Now, do you want to live with your mum or your dad?'

That was a no-brainer.

'My dad,' I told her, without a moment's hesitation.

She had said that whatever I wanted to happen would happen, right? I was still shitting myself in case Mam was hiding behind the door, able to hear what I had said about preferring Dad.

'Okay, your dad it is,' she confirmed.

What a relief. It was back to Nana's house. I was safe. No more smacks, no more living in fear, no more running away. Andrew 1, Mam 0.

Although my dad had won the custody battle, my mam was still entitled to see me every couple of weeks, under the supervision of a social worker. I remember screaming and grabbing hold of the railings so that I didn't have to go. I spent the whole time bawling my eyes out at the very prospect. Meanwhile, I was having the time of my life. I was playing out with my mates; I was getting my clothes washed and my meals cooked. Things were finally starting to look up.

That is, until it was time to see my mam again.

I was playing in the lounge when there was a loud knock at the front door. Every time someone came to the door, I was always nervous in case it was her.

'Andrew,' Nana yelled. 'Your mum's at the door.'

I felt light-headed, as if I was about to pass out. I hurried down the hallway, so that she wouldn't think I was taking too long to answer. The minute I was within arm's length, she guided me across the driveway to her car.

'Get in,' I was brusquely instructed.

My face turned white. Tears welled up at the back of my eyes and I started screaming, hoping that somebody would hear me and come to my aid. Mam ushered me into the back and slammed the door shut.

My Uncle Paul was in the driver's seat, looking confused as hell. He didn't have the slightest idea why I was so unhappy. To him this was a routine visit from a mother to her son, one that estranged parents make every day of the week. Fuck this, I thought, 'there is no way I am going with them'. I balled my hand into a fist and punched Uncle Paul as hard as I could in the back of his head. Some things are worth fighting for.

Uncle Paul had realised something was amiss and turned the car around to head back to my nana's.

'I'm sorry. He isn't happy. I'm taking him home,' he told Mam.

Nana was delighted to have me back.

'You poor thing. It must have been awful for you.'

Yeah, not half. Not many five year olds had been through such emotional trauma. Still, it made me stronger, less capable of feeling pain. Although I was upset at seeing Mam again, I was still very thankful to be living at my nana's house. As far as I was concerned she was the polar opposite of my mam. She was kind, good-hearted and proper respectable, the type of woman who would wear her Sunday best to go to the doctor. It's funny because my granddad was a rum 'un. Whereas dear old Nana had never broken a law in her life, he was a real wheeler-dealer. In fact everything in the house had Belle Vue stamped on the side from when he used to work at the amusement park. I've heard of office workers nicking a few pens from the office but he took things to a different level.

If Granddad had a mischievous side to him he also had a heart of gold. I can still remember the tender way he held me when I was a baby; he was so gentle and caring and the warmth of his embrace has been imprinted on my mind ever since. I felt loved in his arms; the sun was shining and the weather was unusually hot for the time of year. It was the last time I saw him before he died, at the relatively young age of sixty-two. Still, he'd lived a full and active life. He held down many different jobs, fought in the Second World War and stole his own weight in Belle Vue-branded merchandise! Nana was always desperately hiding the cups and saucers whenever anybody came round in case they realised he'd pinched them.

I carried on living with my nana until I was nine. By that time, my dad had met another woman and she was becoming a regular visitor at our house. She didn't bother me to begin with; she did her thing and I did mine. The only problem I had with her during the initial stages of their relationship was her funny name. She was called Thea, short for Dorothea. It sounded like 'fear' and perhaps that was a sign of things to come.

I was shy around her to start off with and I didn't know what to call her. I thought about Mam but then I thought, 'nah, that's not right'. In the end I just called her Thea, not that it made any difference because she would have taken exception to me no matter what I'd called her. It started with a scowl. She would glare at me whenever she could get away with it. It was a particularly callous thing to do, given my life up to that point. I tried to ignore her but, after a while, it got to me. What had I ever done to her? I was a nine-year-old boy, trying desperately to rebuild my life. *She* had walked into *my* life, not the other way around.

As far as I was concerned, she could fuck right off.

After a couple of months of bringing Thea round to my nana's, Dad decided to get a place of his own. He bought a fancy new house five minutes down the road. It was semi-detached with three bedrooms, a front and back garden and a greenhouse. It was pretty posh compared to our old gaff. Still, I would have preferred to have stayed at Nana's, as Thea was a pain in the arse from the minute she moved in. She'd either completely ignore me or pull funny faces to wind me up. Maybe she was jealous of the attention I was getting from my dad. Whatever her reasons, she treated me like a piece of shit on the sole of her shoe.

Shortly after she moved in, Thea fell pregnant and began to treat me even worse than before.

'Keep that bastard away from my kids. I don't want them ending up like him,' she instructed Dad.

Ending up like me? I hadn't ended up like anything yet. I was still a kid myself. Besides, she was hardly a positive role model. She had a mouth like a sewer. If I was with a woman and she had said all that about my son, I would have told her to sling her fucking hook. She wanted to be with my dad and she realised that I came with him. We were a package and she knew what I was like before she got with him. What a cheeky bitch. I still feel angry whenever I think about her. She did her best to eradicate what little self-esteem I had left. She had decided that she was going to victimise me from the get-go. She never called me by my real name. It was always bastard this and bastard that. It was psychological abuse and it fucked my head up. Kicks and punches were easy to take; I understood them. Words were much more wounding.

As the years went by, my life became more and more difficult and I became consumed by hatred and resentment. Every time Thea called me a bastard, I felt like jumping up and banging her. She was getting paid family allowance but she refused to buy me food or clothes and whenever I made myself something to eat, she would shout at me for going in the cupboard. She wouldn't even give me soap but, at the same time, she was calling me a dirty, scruffy, stinking bastard. It was her way of making me feel bad. Cuts and bruises heal but when you're constantly being told you won't amount to anything, it has a permanent effect on the way you think about yourself.

One of the things that really used to bother me was the fact that my Dad never said anything to Thea when she was laying into me. He'd stick up for me when he was alone with her but when I was there he kept quiet and let her say whatever she wanted. One time he was sitting in the kitchen talking to his mates when one of them asked me if I wanted a cup of tea.

'He can't have one,' Thea blurted out from across the room. 'There's no milk.'

I was sitting next to a carton of Stera!

I gave Dad a look that meant, 'Say something,' but he stayed quiet. His mates were looking at him, waiting for him to speak out but still nothing. It was one of the most humiliating experiences of my life.

Thea did her best to make my life as difficult as possible and she even went as far as asking her brother to 'sort me out' at one point, which made me laugh. He was a teacher at one of the local schools and a couple of my mates who were in his class had already told me what a wanker he was. I decided to go round to his house and have it out with him. I pelted his windows with bricks until his pals came out to confront me and then I pelted them with stones until they ran back inside, leaving Wanker on his own at the front door.

'I thought you were going to teach me a lesson?' I sneered.

'I'm going to tell your dad about this,' Wanker threatened, going red in the face.

'Do what you want, you prick,' I told him, and with that I walked away.

The motivation to please my parents declined to the point where I didn't give a fuck. I loved my dad but if he was going to let Thea treat me like this then I was going to rebel. I started wagging school and hanging about on street corners. I stayed out all night to avoid seeing Thea. That was when I first got into solvent abuse. There were only a few of us doing it back then because it was still a new phenomenon. We'd chip in for a tin of glue and then wander around the estate, high as kites, seeing mad patterns in the clouds. It made me numb, like when you're drunk. After a while I'd snap out of it and I'd be delirious, with big strands of glue hanging down my face.

There was nothing like a nice big tin of glue to while away the hours until Dad got up. I felt snidey waking him up to let me in and it was easier to wait until he unlocked the house to go to work. Some of the lads were into drinking and smoking weed but I tended to stick to solvents, mainly because I had drunk a load of whisky one Friday night and puked my guts up. The same thing happened when I smoked my old man's draw; I put it all in one joint and turned myself a nice shade of green.

Glue was the only drug that didn't make me vomit. It got me into trouble with the Old Bill and it gained me a record for breach of the peace but that was the least of my worries. A tin of glue and a fight; that was the definition of a night well spent. I had a lot of pent-up aggression that needed to be released and Gorton had a reputation for gang fighting. It wasn't guns and knives like it is today. It was just different groups of lads having a bit of a scrap. We would hear about other well-respected gangs in the area and compete with them for territory. The Gorton Beano Boys were one of the better-known firms. We wanted to follow in their footsteps.

There were four other gangs that hung about in Gorton at the time: the Market Boys, the Bowling Green Boys, the Reddish Bridge Boys and West Gorton. Altogether the area had a total of two hundred and fifty-odd gang members and, every now and again, we'd all join forces to fight the mobs from Stalybridge and Stockport. I remember when a huge mob of Gorton went to the Shades nightclub in Stalybridge after one of their firm had been putting it about they were going to do us. They were a right bunch of inbreeds. When you live in a place that's as backwards as that, there really is no hope for you.

Determined to teach the incestuous fuckers a lesson, we got a proper big mob together and headed off into their godforsaken little village. There was me, Jimmy Veal, Leo Garvey, Johnny Ryan, Tommy Reilly and a load of other lads but Stalybridge were nowhere to be seen. They were probably too busy shagging their sisters. They weren't even your regular, run-of-the-mill inbreeds; they were a bunch of fucking throwbacks. They all had skinheads and wore Docs and they looked like something from a bygone era. Disappointed by their decision to pussy out, we did a sports shop over instead and headed home in our new Lacoste jumpers and Adidas New York tops. At least we'd gained something from our trip to the back of beyond.

Even when they teamed up with Denton and Guide Bridge, Stalybridge never really stood a chance against us. They came to the Debdale Fair in Gorton and we had them on their toes before they'd even reached the field. They were a firm full of nobodies and the only mob that ever came anywhere near to doing us was Levenshulme. Levy had a couple of handy lads and we ended up teaming up with them to fight with Reddish's firm in Stockport. We always had to travel into our rivals' territory because none of the other gangs would dare to bring it to us. We were more used to defending ourselves than they were because with Belle Vue being in Gorton outsiders were constantly venturing onto our turf.

Clayton and Openshaw both had decent little mobs. Openshaw were only a small firm but they had fifteen game-as-fuck lads. We were the only firm that counted for anything though and I'm not just saying that to big myself up. We really were untouchable. There were articles in the local papers every week expressing concern about

Gorton's gang problem. We were notorious and we enjoyed every last minute of it. We'd been banned from all of the local youth clubs so what else was there to do apart from fight?

Dad was concerned about what I was getting up to while he was asleep and I recently found out that he went to the doctor behind my back to ask for advice about my glue sniffing. I was only thirteen and he was worried I would end up with a habit, although I never did. It was the violence I got addicted to, being part of a gang. We were fighting from dusk till dawn every night of the week.

When you're out all night, you're going to end up fighting with the other kids who are doing the same thing. It's par for the course. We had a laugh though and we used to buzz off people's reactions. I remember when we got invited to a meeting with the local residents after a run-in with some kids from Droylsden. The dibble assured us that no-one was going to get arrested and we were placed in the same room as the lads we were having it with in the hope that we could reach a peaceful solution. It was naïve of the Old Bill to think that a group of twenty rowdy street kids would sit around a table with their sworn enemies and end up being the best of buddies with them. We smashed the place to smithereens and two of us got arrested, despite what the coppers had told us. What the fuck did they expect?

Violence was a hobby but it was also a tool. There are certain situations that diplomacy is incapable of solving, especially when you live in Gorton. When it came to confrontation, I would always stand my ground. My stepbrother David grew up wrapped in cotton wool, which was his mother's fault. As a result he wasn't streetwise and when the other kids on the estate picked on him I had to step in and protect him. I was physically and psychologically numb, which allowed me to put myself in dangerous situations with no concern for personal safety.

David's life was relatively easy compared to mine and so he never became a fighter. Thea used to talk it up, saying that she was going to go out and batter the kids who made fun of him but she was all mouth.

'David,' she'd say. 'You tell all these people who are coming round here bullying you that I'm going go out there and kill them the next time they show up.'

He actually believed her as well.

Even when I was protecting her family, Thea was still a vindictive bitch. I remember when some of the local troublemakers scratched my old man's car. They were stood around Dad, giving him grief, asking him what he was going to do about it. Just to top it off, it was the same bunch of kids that had been picking on our David.

'Oi, knobheads,' I shouted.

I'd been stood behind the garden fence, listening.

'What do you want?' one of the bullies sneered.

'I'm going to fight every single one of you. You can go home and get your brothers, your sisters, your aunties, your uncles, your mams, your dads and anyone else you want to bring. I'll do them all.'

They soon realised that I was most certainly not David.

'You can't come round here doing this and get away with it,' I carried on, and not a single one of them said a dickie bird. They slunk away with their tails between their legs and their eyes fixed firmly on the ground.

My dad was delighted that someone had finally stood up to David's tormentors. He couldn't wait to tell Thea, which was unusual because he'd normally avoid telling her anything that was related to me.

'We've just seen the bunch of wankers who were bullying David,' he told her.

'Oh, what did they say?' she asked, taken aback that he was so jubilant about having come face to face with such nasty characters.

'Well actually, they said nothing,' he grinned. 'Andrew overheard them giving me grief . . . '

Her face contorted at the mention of my name.

'Oh right,' she scowled. 'I bet he did fuck all.'

The cheeky fucking cow. Just because she was a mouthy bitch who couldn't back her words up, it didn't mean she could tar me with the same brush.

'Well let's put it this way. Every last one of them put their head down and walked away. I don't think we'll get any trouble from them lot again,' said Dad.

And do you know what? We never did get any more trouble. Not that she ever thanked me. She was the first one to jump down my neck whenever I did anything wrong but yet she was unwilling to acknowledge anything good that I did.

A couple of weeks later, a similar thing happened when I was out with my stepsister Michaela. We were walking through the estate when a group of kids started making fun of her, shouting abuse across the road. As it turned out, one of them had sold her a brick in a VHS case a few days earlier. They thought it was the joke of the century.

'Is that your boyfriend then?' one of them laughed, pointing his scrawny little finger in my direction.

'Right,' I thought. 'I'm not having this.'

'Are you going to take that shit from them?' I asked Michaela.

'Just keep walking, Andrew,' she pleaded.

'They're a bunch of knobheads. They're a fucking joke. They won't do a thing,' I assured her.

There were three girls and four lads. My type of odds.

'Come on then. Let's have you, you mouthy cunts,' I shouted.

'Please Andrew, don't do this,' Michaela implored, as I picked up a stick, ready to set about them.

'Don't be daft. You should give them a slap yourself.'

By this point the wannabe bullies had left their bikes on the floor and they were backing off down the pavement, scared of what I was going to do.

'Not so brave now, are you? You better come and get your bikes or I'm going to steal them,' I taunted.

They made a few desperate attempts to scuttle forward and grab the bikes before I got a chance to hit them but it didn't work out in their favour. I eventually ended up getting bored and giving them their bikes back. It was funny as fuck and I laughed my head off all the way home. The last laugh was on me though because they ended up putting my dad's windscreen through when I wasn't around.

'Thea says it's your fault,' Dad told me. 'She says you were kicking off with some lads when you were out with our Micky.'

It wasn't my fault. If it had been up to me it wouldn't have got to that stage in the first place.

'Hold on a minute,' I protested. 'I was protecting *her* daughter. Why the fuck is she blaming me?'

If the situation had turned out differently Thea would have refused to acknowledge my involvement. The more she scolded me for things that were beyond my control, the more I wanted to do her in. I had so much anger inside and sometimes I would sit in my bedroom, crying my eyes out for hours, feeling trapped in a never-ending cycle of neglect and abuse. I needed an escape but running away had never solved anything so the only option was to go and stay at my nana's. That wasn't fair on her though. She had just moved house and the neighbours were already beginning to make remarks about how often I stayed over.

That's when it hit me. I could kill Thea.

I was still very young and I'd be out of prison by the time I reached thirty. I might even be able to hold my hands up to a manslaughter charge on the grounds of diminished responsibility. That would mean five years tops.

So there I was at age thirteen seriously contemplating killing my stepmother. I was fully capable of doing it. She'd put me through so much shit that I could have beaten her to death without turning a hair. Then I thought about my nana. How she would feel, knowing that her grandson was doing time for murder? It would have been the talk of the town, with the local busybodies pointing fingers in her direction. No, as much as I wanted to push a pillow into Thea's face while she was sleeping, killing my step-mam was never a genuine option. Nevertheless, the mere fact I could have done it made me feel a lot better. She was only alive because I was allowing her to live and from that moment on, nothing she ever said to me had any effect. She was at my mercy and if she pushed me too far, I could always bang her out. For the first time in my life, I felt truly powerful. Whereas other kids my age would have been forced to obey, I was free to do as I chose.

And, what's more, I was about to discover my true calling.

2

THE LEGENDARY YOUNG GUVNORS

I have no idea why I originally chose to support the Blues because everyone at Varna Street, where I went to school, followed United but blue just seemed like the right colour to wear.[1] I was an awkward bastard and I wanted to stand out from the crowd, although when I got a little older, I realised the significance of my choice. City were the underdogs but I didn't want to be like everyone else. I wanted to back the horse that the other punters had underestimated. United were all about the money, City were a proper working-class team with humble beginnings. Their origins mirrored my own situation to a tee.

I remember the first game I went to. I'd been bugging Dad to take me to a match for weeks but he seemed determined to put it off. 'I'll take you next week,' he'd tell me. Yeah, right. After a couple of months of hardcore pestering he finally agreed to take me to see the Manchester derby, at Maine Road, on 13 March 1974, which ended in a goalless draw. It was the first time I'd ever seen grown men singing and it was weird as fuck.

I was in awe of the number of people who were there and there was a ritualistic element to it, as if we were held together by tribal ties, chanting and waving our scarves as a way of celebrating our common bond. People were swearing, shouting things like, 'Fuck that. You should have scored, you twat.' They were passionate about their team

---

[1] It was strange that most of West Gorton, where a good number of my classmates were from, supported Man U, seeing as it was the birthplace of City. United must have somehow managed to establish a grip on the area over the years.

and it was infectious. At first I thought, do I fit in here or not? I still didn't trust people, which was understandable given everything that had happened to me. But, after a while, I let my guard down and started to relax. It was a very accepting environment and, as long as you were supporting City, you were one of the lads.

After the match, I got my first taste of football violence. My dad was taking me to the car when we came across a group of older fans with long hair and flared trousers, going at it hammer and tongs. It was the first time I had seen adults fighting and it was a sight to behold.

'Come on,' Dad told me. 'They're just a bunch of idiots.'

They didn't look like idiots to me. I was impressed. I'd seen wrestling on the telly but it was nothing compared to this. The other kids looked terrified but I wasn't frightened. It was something new, something exciting. I remember thinking, 'fucking hell, you don't see that every day'.

'What was that about?' I asked Dad.

'It was nothing,' he replied.

But he looked worried and added. 'Don't worry. As I say, just a bunch of idiots.'

It didn't look like 'nothing'. There were police running around and flashing lights and people dragging their kids around the corner to safety. My old man has never been one for violence. He's a proper straight goer. He didn't approve of it then and he doesn't approve of it now. Still, the more he attempted to skirt around the day's events, the more fascinated I became.

From that day on, I went to as many games as I could. I'd go with Leonard Taylor, another wayward young lad. We took the piss out of people on the bus and spat and threw coins at the away fans on the way to Maine Road. It was never enough though. We had an insatiable desire for trouble and lobbing a bit of loose change at the other side could never quench it. Eventually, we decided to hang around after a match to see if there were any other opportunities for getting up to mischief. It was a move that would change our lives forever. We encountered organised hooligan gangs and we knew from the moment we first laid eyes on them that we wanted to be like them.

Initially, we were only on the periphery of these groups. We tagged along with a number of different City firms but we were never involved in the fighting, although that's not to say that we didn't get into our fair share of sticky situations. I remember when we got ambushed by two hundred skinheads at a Norwich away game on 28 August 1982. It was the first time I'd seen cameras at a match. United had been there a few seasons earlier and they'd proper wrecked Carrow Road. The Old Bill must have thought there was a fair chance of the same thing happening again, what with us being from Manchester and all.

We'd just come out of the station at Norwich with a hefty crowd of coppers in tow when we were confronted by a huge mob of shaven-headed hooligans. Our escorts ran for their lives, some help they were. I tried to run alongside them but I couldn't keep up. The next thing I knew, this big, hard-looking East Anglian had come running over to bang me. Luckily, his mate stepped in and told him to leave it out.

'He's just a kid.'

I felt offended that I wasn't seen as a worthy opponent but, at the same time, I was glad that the big cunt hadn't hit me. On the way home, I overheard a group of City lads discussing what had gone off.

'There was loads of them,' this lad was telling his mates, 'and *he* was there.'

Was he pointing at me?

'Did you get caught?'

Fuck, I couldn't exactly tell them that they'd let me go because I was too young to bother with.

'Yeah. This big fella was gonna bang me out but then he stopped.'

Well, it was technically true. I just neglected to mention the reason he hadn't gone through with it.

As we became more and more embroiled in the world of football violence, we began to incorporate elements of hooliganism into our local gang. Whereas we had previously gone unnamed, we decided to call ourselves Gorton the Business, inspired by the calling cards that were distributed by some of the other mobs. At this stage, we were still fighting with groups of kids from the neighbouring estates. It didn't matter what team they supported. We were defending our territory from invading hordes.

My decision to become a full-time hooligan coincided with City's relegation at the hands of Luton Town on 14 May 1983. We were neck and neck with them going into the last game of the season and needed just a single point to stay up. The game was at Maine Road and we were confident that, when push came to shove, we would see them off. But, in the eighty-ninth minute, the unthinkable happened: Luton scored and seconds later the ref blew for time up. All our history and tradition counted for nothing; a pub team with a Mickey Mouse stadium had relegated us. I will always remember their manager, David Pleat, running onto the pitch in a stupid white suit with his arms held high in the air. He looked a right twat and if he'd known what was going to happen next he might have thought twice about being such a smug cunt.

The entire stadium erupted into violence and a huge mob of City fans descended onto the pitch, intent on killing Luton's players. Pleat's face quickly turned whiter than his suit. There had only ever been a small contingent involved in the violence at the other games I'd been to but this was a full-scale riot. They had to bring mounted police onto the pitch to escort the Luton players off. I was right in the thick of the action, loving every single minute. City had been relegated but I didn't give a fuck. I'd been promoted to the top league of football hooliganism. I was no longer a spectator. It was my time to shine. Fists were clenched, bricks were hurled and tempers were frayed.

After the match, I remember seeing two black lads running down the street carrying a white Sergio Tacchini tracksuit they'd robbed off with during the mêlée.

'Who's having the bottoms and who's having the top?' one of them asked.

'Well I want the bottoms,' the first lad replied.

I could sense a row brewing.

'I'll fight you for them,' his mate responded.

Within seconds, they were rolling around on the floor, kicking the shit out of one another. While they were busy pummelling each other's faces, I quietly snuck in and grabbed the top. It beat having to fight them for it and anyway I'd already done my fair share of that on the pitch.

The next morning, I awoke to find my face plastered all over the *News of the World*. One of the centre pages showed some of the lads stood around Luton's goal scorer, ready to beat the living fuck out of him. It was my first taste of infamy. I stuck the picture on my wall and it stayed there for months. It was the ultimate trophy. I had fought for my team and had the photos to prove it, published in a national newspaper for all to see.

After a couple of days, the fact we had been relegated from the first division began to hit home. Up until about 2008 and the takeover by the Abu Dhabi investors, the average City fan didn't know what it was like to see the team doing well but I was lucky enough to have a brief glimpse of it before success was cruelly snatched away. For many years, we would carry on being shit, bouncing up and down from the top tier of English football to the second and even the third division. We eventually managed to work our way back up the leagues but we were never going to be the same again. Still, that's what being a loyal supporter is all about. You keep on going even when your club are losing.

The pitch invasion after the Luton debacle sparked a desire in me to be a top lad. I was sick of being a bit player. I wanted to be the star, and so I started knocking about with the two main City firms: the Cool Cats and the Kippax Boot Boys. There would be no more watching from a distance.

Just because the two firms followed City it didn't mean that they saw eye to eye on everything. There was a lot of racial tension in the air. The Cool Cats were mostly black lads from Moss Side and the Boot Boys were 100 per cent white. I didn't understand race back then. It was a bit over my head. I remember seeing people carrying National Front placards and wondering what they were on about. I'd be thinking 'Fucking hell, it always seems to be kicking off around Rusholme. I wonder what that's all about.' Looking back, the blacks and the Asians got a lot of grief and it was a way of keeping the working classes divided. As far as I was concerned, blue was the only colour that made the blindest bit of difference.

The black lads[2] were younger and naughtier than the white firm.

---

[2] I say 'black lads' as the majority of them were black, although there were always a couple of white lads knocking about with them. Scouse, Simo and Lukes spring to mind.

They'd get up to more mischief and they'd steal things from shops on the way to matches, which was of course something I could relate to, as I'd been thieving for years. The blacks were into the same things I was into and while the white kids formed an exclusive club, I hung about with both races, refusing to choose between the two groups.

The Cool Cats used to proper buzz off me. I was a thirteen-year-old white kid who would stand my ground with them and they all thought that it was hilarious. I would regularly walk into Moss Side on my own, even though people would tell me, 'Oh you can't go there, it's rough as fuck.' But I never had any problems. I had more trouble walking round the white areas of the city and I always thought that whites who didn't like blacks were arrogant bastards with a superiority complex.

The Cool Cats knew that I didn't have a racist bone in my body and the same went for the majority of the younger generation. It was the older hooligans who made a person's race an issue and so, as time went by, our mob became progressively less divided and we trans-formed from two separate, racially determined factions into a single unified firm. It got to the point where we were battering the National Front on behalf of the black members of our mob. Those cunts came to Maine Road handing out fliers and we beat them black and blue and told them never to show their faces again. We didn't give them an explanation. We just said, 'We don't want you here so do one, dick-head. You're not Man City and you're nothing to do with football, end of. You can't come here doing that. Try it again and see what happens.'

You could be black, white or pink but if you were City, and you came with us, that was it. We didn't need that fucking nonsense. When five hundred United are steaming in and there's fifty of you stood there, some of them black, you don't want racist people with you, simple as. It causes tension and it fucks with group cohesion.

At first, it was only ever the white lads who would go to away games. That put us at a major disadvantage. In the lower leagues we were going to places like Barnsley and Huddersfield and the whole town was turning out, expecting a big club like City to have a hefty mob. I remember taxi drivers jumping out to get us and the first time I went to Barnsley, there were old ladies throwing pieces of coal at us. We went everywhere with our team and, everywhere we went, we got battered. We were completely disorganised. It was a case of whoever turned up turned up. There was no forward planning.

After a year of getting twatted, we decided that enough was enough and we began to plan each game in advance. United had been going abroad and smashing Europe up for the last few years. They had a rep to their name and we needed to compete with them.

From that day on, we took a mixture of white and black lads with us to every match. By that stage, we were not only double-game but also clued up from the scraps we had been in over the last year. It had been a great learning curve. We'd been battered but at the same time we'd gained a lot of experience from watching other firms going to work on us. This time round, we were unstoppable. We went through the whole second division, beating other mobs to a pulp and cementing our reputation as one of the country's top firms. We went to Leeds and turned them over, we went to Carlisle, Newcastle, Chelsea, Sheffield. . . we did them all over and nobody bothered us. It was too easy. We were young, we were fit and we were crazy.

By the time we'd worked our way back up to the first division in 1985 we knew exactly what we were doing and we were willing to stand our ground against anyone. It was a good job too because we were about to have it with the likes of United and West Ham and they had some naughty people in their mobs. If we'd have come up against them back when we first became involved in the scene we would have been shitting ourselves.

Now that we were a top mob, it was time to become more professional. The first thing we needed was a name. All the other firms had their own calling cards and there was no point going against another mob if they didn't know who they were fighting with. 'How about the Minibus Mafia?' one lad suggested. We got the train to most games so that wasn't even accurate. Another kid got some cards printed up with the slogan: 'We're the Beer Monsters. You've just been tuned in by the Beer Monsters.' That was even worse than the Minibus Mafia suggestion. 'Alive in 85' was the next proposal. That was hardly likely to be long lived. What would happen in 86?

After being known by several different and equally shit names, we decided to go for something that would show that we were a lot younger than the other mobs, West Ham had opted for a similar concept. They were called the Under 5s but that was a crap name. It was like being called the Nursery Boys or the Prepubescents. We were after something that would let the other firms know that a bunch of kids were about to take their title from them.

'How about the Young Guvnors?' I ventured.

The Cockneys were always going on about how they were the 'fackin' guvnors' so I thought, 'wait a minute, *we're* the fucking guvnors'. It was our way of saying: 'hang on, you think you're in charge but that's only because we haven't played you yet'.

Young Guvnors it was.

The Guvnors consisted of fifty main members and countless stragglers and hangers on. I wouldn't say we had a leader but Spinner, Lee, Rowan, Frankie and Rodney and I were usually at the centre of what was going on. I had the rail card so the rest of the mob relied upon me to get from A to B.[3] That gave me a certain degree of power, not to mention the fact that I was known for being a rum cunt. You can get a lot more done with a small, tight-knit group than you can with a big mob and we had each other's backs covered no matter what.

The English are renowned for rioting. We're repressed and uptight to the point where we feel the need to go completely wild every now and again and so the Guvnors were carrying on an age-old tradition of recreational violence. When you're uneducated, with no financial backing behind you, the only power you have is in your fists. What money does for the middle classes, brute force can do for the working classes. It's our legacy, handed down through generations of second-class citizens. I could never afford expensive clothes or trainers but I had the power to smash the fuck out of a shop window and take them. It was our way of bridging the divide.

Smash and grabs were an easy way of getting money for the game. On the way to games we'd put a brick through the window of a sports

---

[3] In those days, the best way to scam the trains was by using a family railcard. So long as we had one, four children were allowed on for a quid each with every adult. We got every fourth lad to buy a ticket and the rest of us told the inspectors we were their kids.

shop and grab ourselves gear worth £50. While a lot of the lads would steal things to sell on and make a profit, I was thieving so that I wasn't forced to wear the same pair of clothes again and again and so that I could afford to go to matches. I'm not saying what I was doing was right but desperate times call for desperate measures. I didn't want to be the kid with holes in his jumper and stains on his trousers. That was degrading. Nicking went hand in hand with being a hooligan. We didn't attack innocent people and we weren't into robbing old ladies or bullying anyone weaker than us but, apart from that, anything went.

Commercial burglaries were another easy earner. I can still remember the first one I did. It was a massive factory with loads of interesting little nooks and crannies. I wasn't nervous. I knew that no-one was around and that I was free to go about my business without having to worry about anyone clocking me. House burglaries were scarier because there was always a chance of the occupants coming home and catching you. In principle I don't agree with breaking into people's houses but you have to remember that no-one had ever taught me right from wrong.

The first time I burgled a house, I did it to impress my mates. I didn't stop to think about the moral implications, although you don't when you're that age. I put a piece of wet cardboard over the window so that it would muffle the sound of the glass smashing and, five minutes later, I had come away with £320 and two thousand four hundred-odd cigarettes. We split our earnings between the group and I ended up getting £80 and sixty cigs. I bought trainers, a jumper, a pair of jeans and a tin of glue; £80 went a long way in those days.

There I was breaking into people's homes to get money to buy clothes and, at the same time, my teachers were laying into me for not turning up at school in the correct uniform. It made me realise just how hard I had it compared to other kids my age. How can you expect someone to live an honest life when their belly's rumbling and they have nothing to eat? If you're in that situation you're going to rob no matter what your personal morals dictate.

My teachers pissed me off. A lot of the other kids were taught to be scared of things at home. They'd get told, 'you can't do this and you can't do that, you've got to be wary of these people and you've got to put on a show for them'. It was nothing to do with what was right or wrong. It was more to do with their parents worrying how people would perceive them. Thea saw me as a piece of shit no matter what I did and so my attitude was fuck her and fuck school. Teachers are used to you bowing down to them as soon as they've said, 'You, boy,' but I wasn't bowing down to anyone, let alone some power-hungry wanker trying to teach me subjects that I wasn't interested in learning.

I remember them trying to demonstrate the art of pottery. How the fuck was that going to benefit me? Sensing that I couldn't care less what he was saying, the teacher got frustrated and threw a piece of clay at me in a last-ditch attempt to get me to pay attention. 'Fuck you,' I told him. 'I'm out of here.' And as it turned out, that was the last I saw of him for three months. I was off to a place that made my school days seem like a walk in the park. It was the era of Maggie Thatcher's 'short, sharp shock' treatment and it was time for me to learn a very different set of lessons.

I had been accepted at the University of Crime and there was no bunking off.

3

A SHORT, SHARP SHOCK

'Andrew Bennion,' the judge addressed me. 'You have been convicted of the serious offence of burgling a domestic dwelling. I have no choice but to issue you with a custodial sentence.'

It was only my third house burglary. I was thirteen at the time. I hadn't stopped to consider that I might get caught. I thought: 'Okay, I need food, I need clothes and I need glue to keep me warm. If I rob this house then I can afford all three.' If I'd been aware of the consequences of my actions I would have stayed well away.

Nowadays they try to avoid sending children to jail. It is recognised that it does more harm than good, but the prison system was a lot more punitive in those days and they didn't care so much about rehabilitation. If you did something wrong you had to pay for it. They were into military training and they wanted to break down your will-power and force you to conform.

Anybody who claims that they weren't worried about their first time inside is a barefaced liar. The journey to Whatton detention centre[4] was

---

[4] HMP Whatton is now a rehabilitation facility for sex offenders. In November 2006 it was revealed that £5,000 of the annual budget was spent on cash prizes for the nonces' bingo sessions. I'm sure that the people of the picturesque village of Whatton in Nottinghamshire are pleased to have eight hundred sex beasts living on their front doorstep, especially when the money that is being spent on 'curing' them is being allocated in such a sensible and well-thought-out way. Back when I was in there, the centre was used to house good, honest criminals. To the best of my knowledge there weren't any paedoes in there; they would have got their heads kicked in.

proper nerve-wracking. I was cuffed to this other lad in the back of a car and the screws were taking bets on how long we would last.

'He looks fairly sturdy,' one of them said. 'I'll give him a month.'

It was their attempt to shit us up so that we would be easier for them to manage but it was counterproductive, as it made me hate the system even more.

The centre was a big, imposing building with luminous yellow lighting and eighteen-foot razor wire on the perimeter. It was fucking intimidating and I remember thinking 'wow, this is the real thing'. It looked like an army base and the screws seemed to think that they were in the SAS. The minute I walked in, this sadistic, military-looking cunt started barking orders.

'Name?' he bellowed.

'Andrew Bennion,' I told him.

Whack! He slapped me hard across the face.

'Name?' he yelled, getting redder in the face.

Was this guy thick or something? I'd just told him my name.

'Andrew Bennion,' I repeated.

Whack! He slapped me again. What the fuck was up with this fucking idiot? Was he deaf?

'Sir!' he shouted. 'It's sir.'

'Okay,' I thought to myself, 'whatever it takes to stop you slapping me.'

'Name?'

'Andrew Bennion, sir.'

I spent my time inside getting ordered around by wannabe sergeant majors who got their kicks from slapping a bunch of kids around. Every morning I was woken by a smart-arse screw trying to play the funny cunt.

'Rise and shine. Hands off your cock. Come on, let's have you.' They were constantly trying to get a rise out of us. It was bad enough waking up in a strange environment, surrounded by barbed-wire fencing. Still, I'd been through a lot worse and come out of the other side.

One of the few times we got to show our defiance was when we were playing footie against the guards. It was our chance to show them that we were just as good as they were, although they didn't take kindly to being beaten by young lads. Four weeks into my sentence, I made the fatal mistake of saving a shot from one of the more ill-tempered screws. He grabbed my hand and twisted it back as far as it would go, causing me to drop to the floor in agony. I had broken my wrist in three places a few months earlier and it was held together with metal pins.

'On your feet, boy.'

He grabbed my ear and dragged me up onto my tiptoes. And this was the fella who was supposed to be setting a good example. What a fucking scumbag. As it turned out, the bullying bastard had bent my hand back so far that I had to go to hospital to have it looked at. Screws are like coppers; there are good ones and there are bad ones but the vast majority are rotten to the core. I got a taxi to the hospital, accompanied by another equally horrible prison guard. It was a ball ache having to see the doctor in a pair of handcuffs. I felt a right thug.

'There are a couple of comics in the back,' the cabbie told me. 'You can read them if you want.'

It was refreshing to be spoken to as if I was a human being, rather than a piece of shit on the bottom of somebody's shoe.

'He can't have comics,' snapped the sour-faced warder sitting next to him.

He could have shown a little sympathy given that it was his lot who had caused me all this hassle in the first place. It didn't stop there though. When we arrived at our destination, the nurse offered me a cup of tea and he barked an order at her not to give me one.

'He needs to have something warm to drink if he's going to have an X-ray,' she told him.

She was lying, of course. Looking back, she probably had a good idea of how I'd received my injuries and felt that she needed to look after me as best she could.

'Well he can't have any sugar then,' the screw instructed her, determined to deprive me of anything even vaguely pleasurable to drink.

'Okay,' she told him, pretending that she would carry out his instructions.

She left the room and returned with a steaming-hot cup of tea and it was either the sweetest tea that I've ever tasted or she'd snuck a sugar in there on my behalf.

I was the last one left in the waiting room and I have an inkling that the nurse deliberately held me back so that I'd be able to spend as much time as possible in the outside world. When it was time for me be seen, the doctor told the guard he'd have to take my handcuffs off so that the metal didn't interfere with the X-ray machine. By this point it was obvious that the staff were firmly on my side and, fair play to the doctor and the nurse, they made my time at the hospital as comfortable as possible.

All in all, it wasn't a bad day out. If I'd have gone in towards the start of my sentence I would have been tempted to do a runner but I only had a couple of weeks left to do and it was good to see ordinary people going about their business. It reminded me that there was a world outside the detention centre.

Luckily, my wrist wasn't too badly damaged, although that's not to say it didn't hurt like fuck. It's easy to play the hard man when you're in charge of a group of fourteen-year-olds. If he had done that to me in adult prison he would have had a major problem on his hands.

The next few weeks passed quickly. Now that I had been given a taste of freedom, I was raring to get out. I was glad to be returning to the real world, although to say that I was even slightly rehabilitated would have been a blatant lie. I'm not the type of person who responds well to bullying and if somebody tries to get a message across by repeatedly bellowing it down my ear I ignore them.

To save them the effort of having to ferry me back to Gorton, the staff at Whatton issued me with a rail card and dropped me off at Nottingham train station. Within a couple of minutes of being set free, I'd spent my discharge money on cigarettes and I was sitting on the train, sparking up a fag. I was still two years below the legal age to smoke; so much for me being a reformed character. It was a long journey and I had to change at Stoke and Derby. I must have set off pretty early because I was back in Manchester for eleven.

The main effect of being locked up was that the authority figures in my life now seemed tame compared to the screws. Why would I be afraid of a schoolteacher when I had been faced with a carbon copy of Colonel Kurtz, intent on breaking my spirit? I'd had no choice but to follow orders for the past three months. I had been locked in a dormitory and surrounded by eighteen-foot, barbed-wire fences. Now that I was free to walk away, did they really think that I was going to carry on letting them tell me what to do?

'You know what?' I said to myself, 'I'm not going to school anymore.'

And from that moment on, I avoided going in at all costs. Every year, my school report said the same thing: 'Don't know him. Can't comment.' I only went in twice in the whole of the fifth year, once on the first morning of the first day and once on the last day to collect my leaver's certificate.

Thea used to kick me out of the house every morning at eight o'clock, regardless of whether I was going to school. It didn't matter if it was raining, snowing or hailing. It was becoming increasingly difficult for us to carry on living under the same roof. As I'd already decided I couldn't kill her there was only one other option. It was time to move out.

I was fourteen and too young to get a place of my own so I would have to alternate between sleeping at my mates' houses and staying out all night. It was better than living with somebody who didn't care if I was dead or alive. The streets were a better mother to me than Thea had ever been. They looked after me, or should I say, they taught me how to look after myself. If it wasn't for those cold nights huddled around a tin of glue I would never have learnt to defend myself. I'm a product of a harsh environment, a child of the concrete, hardened and moulded by a life of blood, sweat and tears.

Sleeping on the streets was bearable during the summer. In winter I struggled. One time, I had been visiting a friend who lived a fair way away and I couldn't be arsed walking back to Gorton. I decided to sleep in the hallway of a block of upmarket flats. I grabbed the doormat from outside the front entrance and snuggled underneath it to keep myself warm. The following morning, I awoke to the sound of this big burly bloke screaming in my face, telling me that he was going to call the police. He said that he was going to have me arrested for stealing the mat, which was ridiculous, because if that was my intention then why would I have been curled up underneath it?

A few days later, I was sleeping on the platform at Gorton train station when I woke up feeling like I was dying of hypothermia. It was two in the morning and I needed a warmer place to kip. I made my way to a nearby block of flats hoping that there would be a doormat I could huddle under. There weren't any mats but I noticed that they kept their bins in a small shed. There were some loose sheets of newspaper scattered around and so I got underneath and used them as bedding for the night.

I awoke to the sound of the shed door creaking open and an elderly lady shuffling in to put the bins out. Here we go, I thought. She's going to tell me to do one.

'Oh my god,' she screamed.

She looked as if she'd seen a ghost. Before I had a chance to explain to her that I had nowhere else to go, she had darted off down the street with a look of terror etched across her face. Well, I thought, it beats her accusing me of stealing the newspapers.

Two minutes later, the lady gingerly poked her head round the door and let out an almighty sigh of relief, as if the weight of the world had been lifted from her shoulders.

'I thought you were dead. Wait there. I'll get you a nice, warm cup of tea.'

It was funny how the woman from Gorton had gone out of her way to help me, whereas the fella in the posh block of flats was more concerned about his precious doormats than he was about the fact that I had been reduced to sleeping on the streets. You can have all the wealth in the world and still be a complete bastard.

I learned a whole range of tricks for keeping warm in the winter. I would climb inside a supermarket skip and cover myself with cardboard, using the flattened boxes as makeshift bedding. I had to be careful not to oversleep and end up getting emptied out with the rubbish the next day though.

Most of the time, I'd find an abandoned building in which to shelter. It was rare that I slept in the open air. Sometimes I'd camp out on the wasteland near Gorton reservoir and light a fire to keep warm. I had bought myself a sleeping bag for £9 and it gave me great service over the years. There would usually be other people around the reservoir until about two in the morning so I'd only have to spend a couple of hours on my own. At eight, I would go round to my nana's for breakfast. This continued until I was old enough to get a place of my own.

The dibble didn't like us wandering about at night and they did their best to make our lives a misery. They'd either move us on or arrest us for breach of the peace for glue sniffing. It wasn't a crime back then, it's only recently that it's become illegal for underage kids to inhale solvents. The police tactics were proper strange because they'd haul us down to the station, charge us and give us our glue back on the way out. If they wanted to stop us getting high they would have confiscated it, so they were just trying to make things difficult for us. We were always getting legged about the place and if it wasn't for me and my mates then they wouldn't have needed half as many coppers on the beat in Gorton.

The Old Bill should have been thanking us, not arresting us. We made sure they never had a dull moment. I remember when a couple of us were up a tree in the local park stoned off our heads and a group of dibble stood directly underneath. Solvents make you drool and one of the lads couldn't keep the spit in his mouth. The next thing I knew, the cops were covered in a long string of saliva and we were bolting across the park.

Another time, me and a few of the lads skipped a court appearance after being brought in on a shoplifting offence and we decided to pitch a tent in the middle of a bowling green. We were rudely awakened by the park keeper, telling us that we shouldn't be there and threatening to call the police.

'Okay, okay,' I told him.

If the Old Bill had turned up they would have had us for failing to attend court. We moved our tent to the valley next to Gore Brook and camped out there for the next few days. Everyone in Gorton knew where we were apart from the Five-O. All the local teenagers were coming down to the brook to sit around sniffing glue with us.

The social services knew that I was staying out all night but there was nothing they could do. They were aware of what my home life was like and they probably thought that the streets were the best place for me. They didn't have the right systems in place at the time and Gorton was notorious for the amount of feral kids who walked the streets after dark, off their heads on all types of different illegal substances. So long as the children of the councillors and council officers were tucked up in their big posh houses, they couldn't have cared less about us. We were a problem that no-one had the desire to solve, left to our own devices until somebody got their house broken into and they were looking for someone to blame.

Now that I was effectively homeless, I was free to do as I pleased. My dad would criticise me for fighting at the football but there was nothing that he could do to stop me. I was a free spirit. Nobody had the right to tell me what to do. I was surviving by my own hand so I had earned the right to make my own decisions. 'I'm going to the match tomorrow,' I'd gloat when I went round to visit him. 'I'm going to waste someone.' Kids are always trying to big themselves up to their old man. I knew that violence was the one thing he disapproved of and so I told him all the gory details. I'd be excitedly chattering away, describing how I'd beaten people to a pulp, and he'd be sitting there, shaking his head in disbelief.

Football was my saviour. It provided me with structure in the midst of an otherwise chaotic life. It wasn't like it is nowadays with people calling themselves 'casuals' and attempting to turn the terraces into a fashion parade. The term 'casual' was a media invention thought up to describe the way that we dressed. We didn't start dressing that way because we were hooligans; hooligans started dressing that way because of us. We were the innovators, never the imitators, and wearing designer clothing was a useful way of distinguishing ourselves from the scarfers. It was a way of letting other mobs know that we meant business. We didn't need to wear club colours to demonstrate our loyalty. We were blue on the inside.

Every worthwhile activity has its fair share of hazards and football violence is no exception. I've lost count of the number of times I've ended up in a police cell. There is any number of illegal activities associated with hooliganism: smash and grabs, shoplifting, ticket touting . . . you name it. One of the best ways of getting designer clothing was to go into a clothes shop, take two pairs of jeans into the changing rooms, put one pair on and then take the other pair back. You could cut the electronic tag off with wire cutters and fuck off home with the gear. If

I wanted something, and it would fit in my coat, I'd have it. Most of the time though I'd only steal the things I needed, with food, clothes and glue my three priorities.

Ironically enough, my first ever nicking at a match, in March 1984, was for something that barely registered as a crime. We had managed to jump the train all the way down to Brighton and we were proper made up about it. The problem was that we had fuck all money and needed to find a way into the ground. ''Ere Benny,' one of the lads shouted, waving his hands around and signalling desperately for me to come closer. He was gesturing frantically in the direction of the bloke in front of us. That's when it hit me. There was a large, white envelope hanging out of his pocket.

'Right, I'm having that,' I said to myself. I grabbed hold of it and shoved it down the front of my trousers. The owner of the envelope continued down the street, oblivious to the fact he had been robbed.

There were a good hundred tickets crammed inside the envelope. The bloke we'd stolen it from must have been some kind of match official. Even if we sold the tickets for a fiver apiece, we'd end up netting £500. This was 1984 and half a grand was a lot of money, especially for a fifteen-year-old. I have never been particularly material-istic but I saw pound signs flashing in front of my eyes. And, out of the corner of my eye, a sudden flash of navy blue.

Shit, it was the Five-O. They had the robbery victim with them and he was looking right at us. We were fucked.

Brighton police force are a bunch of shady fuckers.

'Just admit it. You'll be on the next bus home,' they said.

Yeah, right.

'No comment.'

If I didn't answer their questions I wasn't likely to incriminate myself.

'Where were you shortly after ten this morning?'

What was the point in asking that? I was hardly going to tell them I had been on the same street as the victim.

'No comment,' I repeated.

By this stage, the copper was turning an unhealthy shade of purple but it served him right for trying to pull a fast one. No-one likes a lying cunt.

The coppers eventually realised that I wasn't going to tell them anything and brought a social worker in to talk me round. Usually the social workers would try and get you off, no matter what you had done, but there was something not quite right about this guy.

'Get me a cig and I'll confess,' I told him.

'I'm not too sure about that one,' he stammered.

He knew full well that I was below the legal age to smoke.

'Well, you've got two options. You can either get me a cig or I'm saying fuck all.'

He was becoming increasingly flustered.

'I'll see what I can do. I-I-I can't promise anything though.'

Five minutes later, a copper came in with a cigarette. One minute he's telling people to obey the law and the next he's dishing out smokes to underage kids. What a fucking hypocrite.

'What about my mate? If he doesn't get one, I'm saying fuck all. Confessions don't come cheap you know.'

As if I was going to sell myself down the river for a few measly cigarettes. I had no intention of owning up to anything.

'I'll go and get him one,' the officer sighed.

What a dumb prick. He would have held my cock while I went for a piss if it would have got me to talk.

When I had finished my cigarette the social worker bounded back into the room, grinning like the proverbial Cheshire cat. He gave the cop a sly nod, as if to say, 'I've done what you told me to do'. I could hardly contain myself. I was dying to let the silly fucker know I'd got one over on him. He gestured at me to say something. Did he think that I was going to start spilling my guts now?

'No comment,' I told him.

The copper looked like he was going to blow his fucking top.

'No comment?' he screamed, as it dawned on him he'd been stitched up.

The threat of young offenders meant fuck all to me. I'd been through Thatcher's short, sharp shock treatment and that had been the perfect preparation for anything they could throw at me.

'Time for you to go. You're on remand. You're off to Latchmere House,' the Old Bill informed me.

Latchmere House is now an adult prison but, at that time, it also had a borstal wing. It was in south-west London and most of the other inmates were from the surrounding areas.

'Where are you off to?' I shouted through to my mate.

'Lewes. Somewhere round here.'

It was my first time in youth prison and they could have put me in the same nick as my co-d. But they probably didn't want us to corroborate our stories. It was a bit of a ball ache but it could have been worse. I had some cash on me when I got caught and I managed to shove it down the front of my pants so that the guards wouldn't get onto it. At least I'd have something to trade with once I was inside.

So here I was, facing my second stint inside for a poxy pick-pocketing offence. They tell you that you're innocent until proven guilty but remand is another way of saying that they lock you up until they've decided whether you've actually done the crime. In other words, you're innocent until proven guilty but you end up being punished irrespective of any wrongdoing. Much as I disagreed with being banged up before they had convicted me, I have to admit it was a walk in the park compared to the detention centre. The guards were still a bunch of cunts but I suppose that comes with the territory.

Throughout my entire life, people have always accused me of being a dodgy fucker. Whenever I was round at my nan's house, the neighbours would gossip behind my back and put it about that I was up to no good. I was branded a ruffian, a common criminal who couldn't be trusted. Although I knew they were talking shit, it used to bother me. But it was during this sentence that I would receive the ultimate assurance that there were far worse people in the world than me.

I was about to come face to face with my first murderer.

4

'I'M DOING LIFE MATE. I'M IN FOR MURDER.'

'Eh up Benny,' my co-d greeted me, as he walked into the court buildings. 'How was things in Latchmere House?'

We had been taken from our cells to court so that the judge could tell us whether or not we were going to be granted bail. I had just been told that I was to remain on remand and I was waiting to hear which institution they were going to ship me off to.

'Yeah, not bad,' I told him. 'Not bad at all. How was Lewes?'

His face lit up.

'They're buzzing off you in there Benny,' he grinned. 'I've passed your deps [depositions] around and they reckon you're proper clued up.'

What did he mean by that?

'No comment, no comment, no comment, no comment. . . you knew exactly what to say to 'em.'

'Well,' I thought, 'I am clued up.' I have to admit, though, it did swell my head. At that age, your reputation is the most important thing in the world.

I'd managed to hang onto the cash that I'd smuggled in even though one of the screws had illegally strip-searched me. There's a short set of rules that every self-respecting hooligan should abide by: number one, don't grass; number two, leave the scarfers alone; number three, never turn your back on a mate. What the media never pick up on is that the camaraderie is as much a part of football violence as the violence itself is.

'Here,' I whispered to the other Young Guvnor. 'Have this.'

I slipped him a quid.

Unfortunately, I wasn't as clever as I thought because the guard clocked us and snatched the note out of his hand.

'Where did you get that from?' he bellowed.

The screws at Latchmere House were in a whole heap of trouble. Questions were going to be asked about how I'd managed to get a pound note into jail.

'I'll ask you one last time. Where did you get the money from?'

It was pretty fucking obvious what my answer was going to be.

'No comment.'

The cheeky fucker thought I'd stolen it.

'Right. This will wipe the smirk from off your face,' he told me. 'You're off to HMP Lewes. It's a rough place, Lewes is.'

They couldn't have picked a better place to send me. I was already the stuff of legend in there. They were trying to save their own arses though. They wanted to show that steps were being taken to find out where the money had come from. It was their way of diverting attention away from their failure to search me properly.

HMP Lewes was a grim Victorian prison located seven miles north-east of Brighton. It was an adult jail. They shouldn't have sent me there. There were a few young offenders but it was mostly adults. I was used to petty criminals but there were some seriously dangerous people in Lewes.

'How long have you got then?' I asked this big tattooed guy in an adjoining cell.

'I'm doing life mate. I'm in for murder.'

'Fucking hell,' I thought, 'I'm not coming out of my cell again unless I have to.'

Bang! Those heavy steel doors make some fucking racket.

'Time to get your food,' growled an equally heavy-set screw.

I was edgy as fuck after my run-in with the killer. Still, there was no point in hiding away. I had to eat and so I grabbed my plastic cutlery and headed down to the bottom landing.

From reading a lot of other hooligan books, I've come to realise that one of the genre's major failings is that nobody ever admits their weaknesses; everybody is fearless 100 per cent of the time. Life of course isn't like that and I can tell you that the moment I realised who was dishing the food out, I went as white as a fucking sheet. It was the murderer. I carefully avoided eye contact, quickly collected my meal and scurried back to my cell. Fortunately, I was due in court the next day as I had applied for bail again and I got remanded back to Latchmere House, which, despite being a tough nick wasn't quite on a par with Lewes.

I was eventually granted bail and remanded into the care of the local authority. They had originally told me that I was going to be flown back to Manchester but the judge wasn't happy about me travelling unattended. To be fair though, the care home was actually fairly pleasant. I had my own bedroom and they even provided a little spending money. If I had stayed for a few more weeks, they would have given me a couple of hundred quid to spend on clothes. I should have confessed to something else so that they kept me in for longer! In the end I was only there for a couple of days. They were able to find a social worker fairly quickly and, the next thing I knew, I was on my way back to Gorton to sign on at the police station.

Although I was glad to be going home, I was still waiting to find out the sentence for nicking the tickets. I had an eight-till-eight curfew and I had to go and see the Old Bill every day up until my court date. At least I would end up in a local prison if they decided to lock me up again, which was better than being sent back to Latchmere. They'd already shunted me around to three different institutions and I wanted to get the whole thing over and done with.

'Andrew Bennion,' the judge addressed me. 'You are to remain in the care of the local authority until you are fit to re-enter society.'

It didn't look good. My mate had got off with community service.

'You are to be taken to Rose Hill in Northenden, where you will reside until further notice.'

They had issued me with a care order, which meant that they had the right to keep me in the custody of the state until my eighteenth birthday. I'd been to a detention centre, a young offenders institute and an adult jail and now I was off to my second care home.

Rose Hill was similar to the first home they put me in. I could smoke, there was a pool table and we were allowed weekly visits. Dad came to see me every week and brought ten cigarettes to keep me going until the next time I saw him. The other lads were a mixture of remanded juveniles and kids whose parents couldn't look after them. Some were innocent and others had committed the most serious crimes imaginable. There was a black lad who had been accused of killing his teacher. He had supposedly stabbed her to death and hidden the body in a cupboard. He was always all right with me though. Everyone has their breaking point, I suppose.

Although the regime at Rose Hill was relaxed compared to some of the other institutions I'd been in, there were still a couple of unsettling features. They had this crazy Scottish night man who would go around whacking people with a towel rack; he was a right mad cunt.[5] Then there was the fact that they would wake me up early every morning and force me to go to school. They had an on-site classroom, which made it impossible to play truant. Luckily for me, my old headmaster did me a massive favour and asked the governor if I could be granted day release so that I could have my lessons in Gorton. I never had much faith in teachers until that point but, fair play to the guy, he went out on a limb to get me back to school. He even told me that I didn't have to turn up in a uniform, so long as I behaved myself in class.[6]

When you're on a care order, they review your case every couple of months. Now that someone had finally shown faith in me, I was beginning to achieve the grades I should have been getting from the start, which would no doubt count in my favour. I was getting As, Bs, the odd C every now and again. I was never a thick kid. I just never saw the point in trying.

'He's made a huge improvement,' my headmaster told the governor. 'He has changed a lot during the past few months.'

The review panel was impressed.

'You've really started knuckling down,' the chairman said.

---

[5] Manchester City Council are thought to have recently paid out millions of pounds in an out of court settlement over claims of abuse at Rose Hill so I guess the Scotsman was the tip of the iceberg.

[6] My high school, Spurley Hey, had been in the news for being one of the worst schools in England so I guess that he was trying to turn its reputation round.

It was one of the few times anyone in authority had ever said a positive word about me.

'Seeing as you've shown marked signs of rehabilitation, we feel it is no longer in your best interests to remain in the care of the state.'

This was it. They were about to grant me my freedom.

'You are free to return to the custody of your father.'

Result: I was finally heading home. I'd paid my debt to society and it was time to let me go.

After being shipped out to so many different institutions, you would have thought I'd have learnt my lesson. And you would be right. I had learnt my lesson – not to get caught. The fact I had refused to tell the coppers anything had cemented my reputation as someone who could be relied on and, if people know that you can be trusted to keep your mouth shut, they're more likely to include you when they go out grafting. In a roundabout way, my pick-pocketing conviction made me more likely to fall in with the wrong crowd.

Most of the crimes I committed were relatively victimless. Now that I was older, I steered away from house burglaries. If I went out thieving, I targeted places that could afford to be robbed, shops and businesses and the likes. The security guards at one of the local shopping centres became so frustrated with our constant shoplifting trips that they offered us regular payments to stay away. It was a reverse protection racket. We hadn't asked them for a penny and, there they were, offering us a wage for doing nothing.

I would say that the majority of football hooligans have dabbled in petty crime at one point or another. Some of the lads were into selling drugs and others made a living from stealing copper and lead from derelict houses. I wasn't one of these who would be out robbing and stealing twenty-four hours a day. If I had enough for cigs, food, clothes and transport then that was all I needed. When you've had no formal education, you have to rely upon your wits and your connections and there's always somebody who will put you onto something. I'm no angel but I'm no devil either and I did what I had to do to survive. I was raised hand to mouth, grafting hard for the bare necessities of life. Yeah I've robbed a few shops and yeah I've done a couple of burglaries.

But ask yourself this. Would you rather I had starved to death?

5

GORE TOWN

For those of you who are wondering whether my living environment was a factor in my descent into crime and hooliganism, I grew up in Gorton, three miles east of Manchester city centre, a place where violence has been a way of life for centuries. Even the name of the area has violent connotations: 'Gore Town'. It comes from a battle between the Danes and the Saxons in which the waters of the nearby brook were stained red with blood. It means 'dirty brook', although to me, blood is the opposite of dirt. There's nothing dirty about it; it's simply the result of people standing their ground and refusing to back down. Over the years, 'Gore Town' became 'Gorton', the forgotten white ghetto of east Manchester. While Moss Side was being hailed as the 'Bronx of Britain' and the 'Chicago of England', Gorton was quietly getting on with being rough.

The dirty brook isn't the only reminder of Gorton's bloody past. Once the Saxons had successfully turned the Danes over, they built a ditch by the side of the stream to keep invaders out.[7] Even back then the gangs of Gorton were defending themselves from rival firms. Fast-forward to the 1840s and we had groups of 'scuttlers'[8] trekking all the way across to Salford to have it with the mobs from round there.

---

[7] Nico Ditch, forming the boundary between Manchester and Stockport and running through Gorton, Levenshulme, Burnage, Rusholme, Fallowfield, Withington and Chorlton-cum-Hardy.

[8] Nineteenth century Mancunian gang members, characterised by their clogs, bell-bottom trousers and long, lopsided fringes.

There were mass brawls involving up to five hundred lads, all armed with knives and hacking the living fuck out of one another.

Hooligans are often depicted as the unwanted scourge of British football. 'Violence has no place in football,' they will tell you, but when it comes to City, the two are inextricably linked. West Gorton FC was originally started in an attempt to provide an alternative to street fighting. Scuttling was at an all-time high and church attendance was at an all-time low and in an attempt to kill two birds with one stone, the vicar's daughter allowed the local people to play cricket on the land owned by St Mark's church.[9] Cricket was only ever played in the summer, leading to it being gradually replaced by football and in return for being allowed to participate the players had to turn up at services to bulk the numbers up. A lot of other churches did the same thing and that's why you have teams called Wanderers and Rovers. They were the teams with no church affiliation so they could only ever play away games. West Gorton FC went on to become Manchester City FC, a club that was set up to provide a sense of purpose to a group of poor, oppressed street fighters.

As the years went by, Gorton transformed itself from a rural township into a large expanse of Victorian terraced housing and although it is no longer under threat from invading hordes of Saxon warriors, its recent history is just as dark as its beginnings. After the decline of the manufacturing industry, gangs of disaffected youths descended onto Gorton's streets and drug abuse became a serious problem. Household income levels fell into the bottom 5 per cent of the country and the crime rate soared. Nowadays its only claim to fame is that it's the location for the Channel 4 comedy series *Shameless*, which is hardly something to be proud of. It is one of the most deprived places in Britain and

---

[9] One of the other reasons behind the church's decision to encourage the growth of St Mark's was the fact that they thought that it would reduce the amount of alcoholism in the city by providing an alternative activity to drinking. Ironically, the main investors in the club ended up being a brewery, which built a brand new ground on Hyde Road in 1887. We originally used to play in black with a white Maltese cross but several of the prominent figures within the brewery were masons and they changed our team colour to blue, as the colour blue symbolises heavenliness in the freemasonry world.

former residents include moors murderers Myra Hindley and Ian Brady, yet another contribution to a chequered past.

However, despite my bleak surroundings, I always knew exactly what I wanted to do with my life. Some kids look up to astronauts or movie stars, whereas others want to be racing drivers or athletes. I looked up to hooligans and I could never understand why the other lads had such unrealistic expectations. How many people actually end up flying a space shuttle or winning a Grand Prix? Not many, especially when you're brought up in a place like Gorton.

My heroes were the type of people who lived around the corner, people like me. I wanted to be a renowned street fighter. It was something tangible, something that I had a realistic chance of achieving. Superheroes on the telly have big muscles and posh uniforms but my heroes weren't much to look at. They wore the same clothes that I wore and they were just normal people. You'd hear rumours about what they'd done and a lot of it might have been bullshit but it was part of their myth. Sometimes you'd walk past them and they'd acknowledge you and you would think, 'Fucking hell, he let onto me. I must know him.' You didn't know them though; they'd just seen you at games and decided to say hi.

When I finally started talking to the fellas that I looked up to, I was surprised at how approachable they were. They were oblivious to the fact that me and my friends all hero-worshipped them. They were ordinary blokes and that was what made them special. There's always a danger that you'll meet the person you've idolised your whole life only for them to reject you but all my heroes accepted me, and it felt good. It reassured me that there was nothing wrong with me. I'd been called a bastard all my life and constantly reminded that I was never going to amount to anything. Yet, here I was, rubbing shoulders with some of the gamest lads in the city.

6

THE ISLE OF MAN

The Guvnors were ahead of their time. We were the first mob to take pictures of rival firms. It was an intimidation tactic, a way of letting them know that we would remember their faces. When the police took photos of us, it always made us feel uneasy so we applied the same principle to whoever we were up against. We were also one of the first firms to use guerrilla-warfare tactics. We were smaller in numbers than a lot of the other mobs so we had to rely on brains as well as brawn. When you're up against a couple of hundred United, and there are fifty of you, you have to outsmart rather than outfight them. We were constantly looking for places to ambush our opponents and gain a tactical advantage.

One of our most memorable battles was on the Isle of Man of all places. City were playing Carlisle, Stoke, Newcastle, Blackburn and Douglas as part of the Isle of Man Football Festival in 1985 and with so many different sets of fans clustered together on such a small island, it was the perfect opportunity for a row. I did an honest week's work so that I could afford the ferry across from Heysham. They had me grafting in a rainwear factory as part of one of those youth-opportunity schemes. My job was to cut the cords off raincoats and seal them in plastic bags, which was fucking mind numbing. To make things worse they'd check to see if you'd done your job properly and send back any coats that still had pieces of cord hanging off. If they expected us to give a fuck about the job then maybe they should have paid us more money, as my wages only just paid for the ticket to Douglas.

On the day that we were due to leave for the festival, City were playing a friendly against Preston. It was an uneventful game and there was no trouble. One of their lads mouthed off at us but that was as close as it came to anything kicking off, despite the fact that we were sat in their seats. As soon as the final whistle went, I was straight on the train to Heysham, mentally preparing myself for the four-hour journey across the Irish Sea.

When we arrived on the Isle of Man, I got the impression that it's one of those places that's basically just a load of countryside with a couple of houses plonked down in the middle. They stage the Manx TT motorcycle races there but, apart from that, there isn't much to do. We sorted ourselves out a hotel and got our heads down, conserving our energy for the week's festivities.

The following morning, a few of the lads got up at the crack of dawn so that they could get a couple of hours thieving in before the tourists arrived. Although I didn't think that there was anything worth robbing, I decided to tag along, just for something to do. We were on our way into the town centre when we noticed what looked to be a vagrant using a Union Jack flag as a makeshift sleeping bag.

'Look at that fella there,' I sniggered. 'He's got a City hat on as well.'

That's when it hit me. The 'vagrant' was the same size and build as Daft Donald, one of the more eccentric characters in the firm. On the one hand he was as daft as a fucking brush but on the other he had been coming with us as long as any of us could remember. And, all in all, he wasn't a bad lad. He just lived by his own rules.

The minute he realised it was us, Donald flung the flag to one side and hurried over to greet us.

'Y'arite lads? Where are we off to then?'

He had stolen the Union Jack from Douglas town hall and the police had spent the morning raiding hotels in a desperate attempt to retrieve it. It was a typical Donald thing to do. He has pulled all sorts of crazy stunts over the years. I remember when he changed his name to Mike Tyson so that he could get round a travel ban. It would have worked but the minute he set foot on foreign soil, he got himself deported for telling the local press he was there to kill some Eyeties.

Donald was living proof that you don't have to be a fashion victim to be a football hooligan. He was six foot two with ill-fitting clothes and a scribbled-out MUFC tattoo on his right arm. He started out as one of their lads but they fucked him off and he started coming with us instead. He was one of those people who's always on the tap. 'Have you got 10p for a train ticket?' he'd ask us. Then when we got to the ground it'd be, 'Have you got 10p for a burger?' or 'Can I have a bite of your sandwich?' If there were any birds about, he'd be straight on their case. 'All right darling. I want to be with you,' was his standard chat-up line. Most of the time they didn't want to know. However, one of his more successful advances ended with him almost getting involved with an underage girl. Luckily for him he stumbled across an under-sixteen bus pass as he was rifling through her handbag. Most people would have quietly upped and left but Donald was determined to let her know that he was onto her.

'You lied to me. I found your bus pass.'

He didn't seem to think anything of the fact that he'd rooted through her stuff to get to it. He had no sense of perspective. As far as he was concerned, he was the innocent victim of a teenage temptress. It never crossed his mind that he shouldn't have been rifling through her bag.

Now that we had the most important member of the firm back on board, it was time to press ahead with the shoplifting. Some of the lads went round robbing the souvenir shops but I didn't see the point so while they were helping themselves to novelty postcards and Isle of Man T-shirts, I was fiddling the slot machines. There are a couple of different ways that you can do a fruit machine over. You can either pop the front off with a screwdriver and help yourself to the cash or you can attach a coin to a strimmer wire and have as many goes as you want. I had spent £40 on my ferry ticket and I was fucked if I was going to miss an opportunity for making the money back.

It was a good thing I hadn't robbed off with anything from the shops because a few of my mates ended up getting their hotel rooms raided. They were given six-week jail sentences, despite the fact that nothing they stole was of any real value. The lads were lucky in a way, because they were still birching criminals, as corporal punishment was practised on the Isle of Man decades after it had been abolished in mainland Britain. Incredibly, it was legal to whip a child with a wooden rod until as recently as 1993.

When we'd had our fill of looting the seafront, we made our way over to the fields where the festival was being held. There was a fella sat at a desk taking the ticket money but I managed to walk straight into the seating area without him noticing.

Of the other firms that were likely to be on the island, we figured that Stoke would pose the biggest threat. But we saw neither hide nor hair of them. It was disappointing, although it left us free to concentrate on robbing the programme money. As soon as the fella had made his way round to us, we were all over the poor cunt.

'Ere, sit yourself down.' I told him. 'Tell us what you think of the match so far.'

Whilst he was chatting away, filling us in on how the game was going, we were dipping our fingers into his takings. Back on the mainland, they would have been wise to people trying to rob off with their money but in out-of-the-way places like the Isle of Man, you could get away with murder. The entire place was designed with thieves in mind.

After the match, we took a walk around Douglas town centre to see if there were any lads we could go at it with. I was still half expecting Stoke to turn up so imagine my surprise when I saw a load of Carlisle bowling towards us, led by this hefty Chinese geezer. We hadn't expected trouble from Carlisle. They were a couple of divisions below us and I knew fuck all about them. I didn't even know where Carlisle was. I knew that it was somewhere in the north-east but that was the full extent of my knowledge. But I've got to hand it to them; they were game. The Chinese fella was as hard as fucking nails and he stood his ground as one of our lads smashed him repeatedly in the face with a steel bucket. He stepped back a couple of paces so that he could regain his composure and then he launched straight back in, throwing punches right, left and centre.

The townsfolk stood around watching our every move, as if we were putting on a show. Given the size of the crowd we'd drawn, you'd have thought the Old Bill would have been on the scene within seconds. But there was no sign of them. I remember thinking 'where the fuck are the Five-O? They should be here by now.' Don't get me wrong, I wasn't complaining; it was just surreal. The coppers in Manchester know what can go off so I was used to the police being all over us the minute we showed our faces. The fact that there was a full-scale riot taking place in a crowded town centre and I had yet to see a single Old Bill was pretty fucking weird.

If anything, I'd say that Carlisle got the better of us in the end. Both firms held their own but they were in the third division and we had expected to walk straight through them. They did themselves proud and I've always rated Carlisle for that. It's a pity we didn't get another go, as the police turned up at their hotel and kicked them off the island. A couple of their lot ended up getting locked up with the City lads who had been caught robbing the souvenir shops. They got on well with each other in jail and looked after each other until they had finished their sentences. With the benefit of hindsight, I realise that the police must have mounted an operation against them. They were easy to find because they were all in the same hotel, whereas we were spread across the town and so it took the Old Bill an extra day to latch onto us. They advised us to leave on the next ferry, and by 'advise' they meant, 'Fucking do it or there will be trouble.'

It was time to endure another four-hour voyage back to Heysham. It was cold and windy and I was knackered. By the time we arrived back at Preston it was three in the morning and we still had a train to catch. And just to top it off, the guy who had been mouthing off at us at the Preston game was stood on the next platform along, trying yet again to wind us up. He had the same set of clothes on that he'd been wearing the day we set off for Douglas so I decided to give him some abuse.

'Change your clothes, mate,' I shouted.

It was stupid o'clock in the morning and we weren't in the mood for chasing after some random mouthy cunt who fancied himself a hard man. We wanted to get home as quickly as possible so that we could catch some shuteye.

Fair do's the Isle of Man isn't the ideal location for a week away but it was something different. It was a good excuse to descend on a quiet tourist spot and add a bit of excitement to the lives of the locals. It wasn't exactly a trip to the Bahamas but, then again, I doubt we could have got away with the same level of mischief in a place that was half-decent, as football hooliganism is a much bigger priority for the Manchester police force than it is for the Isle of Man's Old Bill.

The violence is a fraction of what being a hooligan is about and the Isle of Man Festival was a perfect example of the camaraderie that made the Guvnors a pleasure to be with. It wasn't just a quick scrap with a rival firm. It was a trip on a ferry, it was a day out stealing sticks of rock and daft novelty badges, it was jibbing in, it was Daft Donald waking up under a stolen Union Jack flag. It was a bit of everything, all rolled into one. We were more than just a group of lads who liked to fight with other mobs; we were a family and we had some right adventures together. Carlisle were the tip of the iceberg. We have had it with every firm worth its salt. Hooliganism dominated my every waking thought. For some it was a fleeting phase or a hobby, but to me it was a way of life.

Which was just as well. Because our main foe happened to be the biggest mob in the world.

7

THE RED ARMY

People say we have a bitter rivalry with United because we're jealous of them and I know that's why most people don't like them. But our hatred runs deeper. Let's put it this way: out of all the London firms, our least favourite is Tottenham. They weren't winning anything when our rivalry with them started so what possible reason would we have had to be jealous of them? It doesn't make sense. The reason we hate United so much is because we're a community-based team (or at least we were until recently) and they're a corporate entity. To me they couldn't give a fuck about the football. They're all about the money. Most of our fans live relatively near to the ground, whereas theirs are scattered throughout the country. You can't support a club halfway across the map from you just because of the trophies it has won. You have to stay true to the place you were brought up in, regardless of how well the local club is doing.

Then there's the Munich issue. There are certain United supporters who like to wallow in self pity. The crash must have been terrible for the families of the players who were involved but the fact remains that it boosted United's profile no end. We were the first English club to win a European trophy and a domestic trophy in the same season, but do we get any credit for it? No. Man U got all the shine because people felt sorry for them and they've been milking it ever since. Rather than patting them on the back and telling them that it was going to be all right – as the rest of the country did – we chose to wind them up by singing songs about Munich. Here's one good example, which some people may find offensive:

Who's that dying in the runway?
Who's that lying in the snow?
It's Matt Busby and his boys,
Making all the fucking noise,
They can't get the aeroplane to go.[10]

United can attempt to take the moral high ground but there comes a point when you have to be willing to say, 'Shut the fuck up and stop harping on.' Our Munich chants were our way of telling them we weren't buying into their sob stories and, besides, United sang songs about the Liverpool fans who got crushed to death at Hillsborough and the two Leeds fans who got stabbed in Turkey. The words pot, kettle and black spring to mind.

Man U have always been the first to point the finger. In his book, *The Men In Black: Inside Manchester United's Hooligan Firm,* Tony O'Neill claims that City fans spat on women and children at derby games. That is bollocks. Our shirters might have spat on theirs but our hooligans never did. It's a hypocritical statement to make, as United have been accused of attacking our scarfers. That said O'Neill is a decent bloke. He knew where my house was when I was living in Wythenshawe and he never told the rest of their mob so respect to him for that.

They have always had a massive firm. Our mob was much smaller, so small by comparison that United knew us all by name. They were mostly nameless faces to us and despite their claim that we were nothing to them they never came to Maine Road with anything short of their entire firm. It's easy to play at being a hooligan when you're an anonymous figure in the middle of a thousand-strong horde. Ten of us would have had it with a couple of hundred Red Army if there was no other option but when the boot was on the other foot it was a different story.

One occasion sticks in my mind. It was after a derby game on 7

---

[10] I did warn you. I'm neither condoning nor condemning this song. I'm merely citing it in as an example of what got sung at games. It's not an attempt to make fun of the crash either, as the last thing I want to do is to offend the relatives of the victims. We sang songs about the disaster purely to get United's backs up and there was no ill feeling intended towards any of those who perished.

March 1986, when we bumped into a load of Cockney Reds outside Piccadilly station. We were due to play Chelsea the following day in the league and the Cockneys were giving it the big one, telling us they were going to be on the same train as us and that they were going to give us a proper going over.

'You're dead,' their main geezer sneered across at us, trying to play the hard cunt. 'You're only little boys. We're going to cut you to fackin' ribbons, you mugs.'

He talked a good one and I have to admit that we were intimidated by his aggression.

'Okay we'll see you later then,' I told him, unwilling to let him know how scared he'd made me.

'We're going to rip your fackin' heads off,' he laughed.

He was certainly sure of himself. They must have really been gunning for us. I had a mental image of a hefty mob of Cockney Reds flooding into our carriage, looking to do us in.

When our train arrived, we were half expecting a huge firm of United to pile straight into us as soon as we left the platform. Imagine our surprise when we found ourselves sharing a carriage with a single Cockney Red, and not just any Cockney Red. It was the fella who had been running his mouth off, telling us we were going to get our heads kicked in. He was fast asleep and snoring his fucking back out. It was pretty fucking surreal after all his threats.

'What have we got here then?' I whispered to the rest of the firm.

'Don't disturb him,' one of the other lads smirked. 'Let's wait until he wakes up and then we'll give the mouthy red bastard the fright of his life.'

We positioned ourselves around our sleeping foe and did our best not to rouse him.

'What shall we do once he's back in the land of the living?' another member of our firm asked me.

'We'll teach him not to make threats that he can't back up. He'll get what's coming to him,' I smirked.

A few hours later, the train was pulling up into Stafford station and Sleeping Beauty was finally beginning to awaken. He was pissed out of his skull. He'd obviously passed out because of the booze.

'All right lads?' he slurred. 'I'm Millwall.'

If he was Millwall I was the queen of fucking Sheba.

'Not so brave now, are you?' I snarled, giving him a taste of his own medicine.

'I-I-I don't know what you're talking about,' he stammered. 'I'm telling you, I'm fackin' Millwall.'

Two minutes later, he was lying on the floor with blood gushing from his nose and stars in his eyes. We took his shoes, rifled through his pockets and gave him a couple more digs, just for being a cheeky cunt.

'I'll tell you what,' I told him, 'You can walk the rest of the way back to London.'

And with that, the door was yanked open and he was hurled onto the tracks while the train was still moving.

Luckily for the Cockney, we were only going five miles an hour. The train had been slowing down ready to stop and it was moving at walking pace.

'You fackin' barrrrstards!' he screamed, as our carriage came to a halt at the side of the platform.

Unfortunately for him, there was a copper standing a couple of feet away from us and the British Transport Police don't take kindly to random pissheads yelling abuse at passengers.

'What are you doing down there?' the Old Bill asked him, assuming that he was a drunken idiot who had ventured onto the tracks. 'You'd better have a good explanation.'

'It's not what it looks like,' the Cockney slurred, looking like he didn't know whether he was coming or going. 'I'm tryna get to London. I'm meant to be on that train.'

The copper wasn't convinced.

'Where's your ticket then?' he asked, a look of cynicism etched across his face. I knew where his ticket was. We'd taken it off him when we went through his pockets.

'You bunch of barstards,' he bellowed, enraged that we'd made him look like such a knobhead.

'Well you shouldn't have gobbed off at us,' I told him. 'You were going to rip our fucking heads off a couple of hours ago.'

We could have roughed him up a lot more than we did. He had a couple of cuts and bruises but he got away lightly, all things considered.[11] He had been vastly outnumbered and he'd fucking shat himself, which was ironic given that their firm have outnumbered us at every derby we've ever played. If it was the other way round, and I was surrounded by a group of Reds, I would have fronted them and told them to do what they had to do. I might have reminded them that I was on my own and warned them they were taking liberties but I certainly wouldn't have pretended to be a Millwall supporter. That's the Munichs for you though. They're brave when there's a ton of the fuckers but they go to pieces when you get them on their own.

Our only hope against United was to catch them in smaller groups so that we were evenly matched. We didn't go around picking off lone glory hunters. That's not what football violence is about. The only reason that we did the Cockney Red was to pay him back for being a mouthy bastard. Most of the time we'd target Red Army groups that were a similar size to our own. Sometimes we would scatter them so that we could break their firm down into more manageable chunks. That's what we did when they tried to take the Clarence pub on Wilmslow Road in 1987. We ran them into the estate opposite the pub and spent the rest of the day hunting them down and battering them.

If you can keep your composure, you can often get the better of an opponent even when they've got you outnumbered. One of our most successful battles was in 1986 when the Munichs had West Ham and we were coming back from Liverpool. We'd attempted to have a go outside the Merchants pub on Back Piccadilly but the coppers intervened. We were stood around at Victoria station, talking about what had happened, when we heard a cry of, 'War, War, War.'

---

[11] When it comes to United, nobody can say that we take liberties with them. There have been a number of occasions when we've caught a Red Army lad on his own and we haven't thrown a punch. I remember when we were on the same train as them and half of their lads had to get off to get away from us. Tony O'Neil remained in our carriage sitting quietly as fuck and I just smiled at him and said, 'Y'arite Tone?' Another time, we saw a lad called Joe Brown on Market Street and I shouted, 'All right, Joe?' and waved at him. I met him in prison a couple of years later and he told me he was expecting to get a whack that day. One of United's older lads, Derrick Whittaker, even used to drink at the Cyprus Tavern when we were in there and we never bothered him once.

The next thing we knew, they were on us.

United's firm came running full pelt at us and we were in the process of throwing advertising banners at them when we heard four very scary words.

'He's got a shooter.'

We ran for our fucking lives.

Once I was at a safe distance, I turned around to see one of their mob aiming a silver starter pistol into the middle of a group of City. There was no way of knowing if it was a real gun but it put the fear of god into us. Saying that, we were straight back into them as soon as the barrel had been lowered. In the heat of the moment, you can snatch a split second of rationality here and there but most decisions are based on instinct. I was running on adrenaline and my overwhelming urge to fight was overriding my fear of getting shot. If it was a genuine shooter they had pulled then we were pretty fucking stupid to have carried on scrapping. However, I have a strong suspicion that it was another scare tactic, aimed at backing us off and gaining them time to figure out what to do next.

Whether it was the real McCoy or a replica, the end result was the same. We fucking annihilated them. There were three hundred and fifty of them and a hundred and fifty of us and we wiped the floor with the bastards. You can whip out pistols right, left and centre but if you aren't prepared to defend yourselves then we're going to weigh you in. Simple as. They should have spent more time getting stuck in and less time fannying about with the pistol.

We were buzzing about what had happened because it was proof that United's mob were just the same as the rest of us. They could be beaten. Much as they like to think of themselves as the firm that has never been done, there have been a couple of occasions when we've had a result against them. It didn't happen every week but for them to say we've never got the better of them is a barefaced lie. We've given as good as we've got over the years.

It wasn't only rival hooligans you had to fear on derby day. United's stewards could give you an equally hard time. Give a man a yellow bib and all of a sudden he thinks he has a licence to do what the fuck he wants. Rather than asking us to move, they preferred to push us around, under the mistaken assumption that we would be unwilling to respond in kind.

I remember one game during which the stewards were being right power-greedy wankers. They were manhandling us around Old Trafford something awful and they made the mistake of trying to shove one of our black lads out of their way. Big mistake. Within minutes, we had them cowering in the corner, desperately attempting to shield their faces. You can't go around laying your hands on people and expect them to take it. If somebody tries to grab me then for all intents and purposes they're asking for a fight. The stewards deserved everything they got and we taught them that you either respect people's personal space or you get your head kicked in.

A couple of years earlier, two of United's stewards had allegedly pushed a City fan down the stairs and broken his leg, although they were found not guilty at the subsequent trial. The victim wasn't a hooligan either. He was just your bog-standard scarfer. Give these pricks a bit of power and that's how they behave. I was recently chatting to a couple of Red Army lads and they were telling me exactly the same thing about the stewards. They're a set of fucking scumbags and, if you ask me, they had been asking to get done over for a long time.

It's always useful to discuss things with your rivals and get a second opinion. As far as I'm concerned, people are people and it doesn't matter what side you're on, just so long as there isn't a match on. Much as I hate United and everything that they stand for, I'll be the first to admit that they've had a couple of proper honourable blokes in their firm. I got to know a few of their top faces while I was in jail and they were decent lads, all things considered.

We've had some epic battles with the Munichs over the decades and rather than slate them, I'm going to end this chapter by thanking them for all the top-notch rows. If it wasn't for them, we would never have been able to laugh about the gobby Cockney Red that we threw off the train and we would have been deprived of the sense of achievement we got from defending the Clarence. There was nothing personal in the feud. We just happened to have opposing ideologies. They supported the team that won the most games, whereas we remained loyal to City even though they were shit. Only Millwall–West Ham could come close to the levels of hatred that existed at City–United derbies. That said, over the decades, the hatred has subsided and my feelings towards them have mellowed.

Football hooliganism is like football itself. You hate the other lot in the heat of battle but, when it's over, you go back to your everyday lives and the hatred is put on hold. However, it was sometimes very difficult to control my hatred for one of the other nearby firms, especially when they carved up one of our lads like a piece of meat.

I am talking of course about the Mickeys.

8

THE MICKEYS

There is a town an hour's drive from Manchester where trouble is never far away. Liverpool is Britain's poorest city and Goodison Park, home to Everton FC, is in the heart of Walton, one of its most deprived suburbs. It's a moody-looking place; in fact it reminds me of Moss Side. The buildings are proper old and dilapidated and it's generally horrible looking. Liverpool's ground can be an equally scary place but no thanks to their firm, who are shite. They might have more fans than Everton but when it comes to naughtiness, they aren't even close.

People always try to make out that the two Liverpool firms went to matches together but that's bollocks. Everton turned out for Liverpool's games but Liverpool rarely returned the favour. They were hard pushed to turn out for their own games, let alone anyone else's. Everton were game enough to support the reputation of both the city's teams. They had some nasty people with them and they certainly liked their blades. But it wasn't just knives: they'd use sticks, iron bars, Millwall bricks; whatever they could get their hands on.

Even when they didn't have anything on them, they tried their hardest to make you think that they were about to pull a blade. They'd be dipping their hands inside their pockets every couple of minutes as if they were going to take a razor out and do you with it.

In fact I first became acquainted with Stanley at a game against Everton. I was fourteen. We were playing the Scousers on Boxing Day and I'd just come out of Lime Street when I was set upon and cut. At the time I didn't realise what had happened. I felt a cold, sticky liquid running down my arm and I noticed that my clothing had been ripped. It took me a while to cotton on that I'd been stabbed.

'Look, your top's got a hole in it,' one of the other lads told me.

The blade had sliced straight through my Adidas cagoule and left three small slits in my jumper. Strange as it may seem, I was more concerned about my clothes than I was about being slashed. I'd seen people with scars where they'd been cut up so I knew it was a possibility. It was just one of those things.

The slash marks weren't that big so I didn't bother going to hospital. They were three inches long and an inch wide. My dad wasn't happy but he was used to me coming back from football with bloody noses and the like. My nana was pissed off though. She was left with the task of stitching my cagoule, which she wasn't best pleased about.

The only thing the Scousers loved more than cutting people was talking about cutting people. If you bumped into them on the way to the ground, they'd be saying: 'You're going to get slashed later' and 'I'm going to cut you up, la'.' Whenever you played in Liverpool, there was always a possibility of getting a stripe but if it happened then it happened. Some look down on lads who carry knives but a lot of people still use them and if one of your mates has been slashed, you are not going to stand around saying how out of order it is. You want to get even with whoever did it. You can't avenge someone whose been cut with a blade by using your fists. You've got to respond in kind.

Tit-for-tat slashings were the cause of an intense rivalry between the Guvnors and the Scousers. People say that City hate United because we're shit and they're not. Well how come we hate Everton so much? They're shit as well. We hate them more than we hate Liverpool and they aren't shit. It just proves that our rivalries aren't based on jealousy; they're based on legitimate grievances between our firm and theirs. The main reason we hate the Mickeys is because they cut a lad's throat during what was meant to be a one-on-one at Anfield. It was proper out of order. They lured him round the corner with the promise of a straightener and sliced him from ear to ear.

It was Chrissie James they slashed, our gamest lad by a long shot. He was the same size as I am but strong as an ox. I've seen him knock out three bouncers in as many punches. If anybody ever asks me if I know anyone that could beat Mike Tyson in a fight, I'll point them in the direction of Chrissie and put a fiver on him winning. He's only a little guy but he's got hands like shovels. He's not on steroids either. He's just naturally tough.

One of Chrissie's main weaknesses was that he could never say no to a fight. He had no sense of danger and it was impossible to dissuade him from doing something once he'd set his sights on doing it. We were away to Liverpool in August 1986 when he got cut. Thirty Everton supporters were mouthing off, telling us that they were going to do us in and he took it upon himself to defend our honour.

'Where's Chrissie?' I asked one of the other lads.

'He's gone for a fight with some Scouser. I told him not to but he wasn't having any of it.'

Two minutes later, Chrissie came back, a look of disgust plastered across his face.

'I've been slashed. They never mentioned anything about using blades,' he told us.

There was a copper standing with us and he must have thought that we were winding him up.

'You've not got a mark on you. If you're telling the truth then show me where they cut you,' he sneered.

Chrissie lifted his chin up and a fountain of dark red blood spurted out into the Old Bill's face. Chrissie looked like something out of a horror film. He had a gaping chasm where his throat should have been. The copper looked like he was going to pass out. 'W-w-w-e need to get you to a hospital,' he stammered.

Chrissie was unfazed. He was more bothered that the Scousers had tricked him than he was about the life-threatening injury. It was a sign of things to come. His sense of perspective was rapidly deteriorating and he ended up spending fifteen years in a mental home. The excessive risk-taking was a symptom of his fragile psychiatric state. There is a thin line between bravery and insanity and he was slowly crossing it. It's sad because he's a sound lad and I've known him since I was a kid. Still, it can happen to the best of us. One minute it's all there and the next thing you know, you're in a padded cell with only the voices in your head for company.

From that day on, the Scousers were public-enemy number one. We never got the lad who did it but we turned out in force for every

Liverpool and Everton game and we cut a couple of their lads up in place of him. Saying that, the only person I ever slashed was myself. I bought a 25p craft knife and I ended up catching my hand on it while I was trying to take the cover off. I saw a couple of their lads getting cut though: one of them got his leg sliced open on Lloyd Street when they were playing in Manchester and another got his back carved up when we bumped into them near Euston station later that year before our game with Arsenal. We were in the Lord and Lion pub in Somers Town when one of our lads came running in and told us that a big mob of Mickeys were getting off their train. I was buzzing. Whenever they were in London, you could rely on them for a row. We finished our drinks and set off to meet them.

The minute we got within a hundred yard of the Scousers, they emptied a skip and armed themselves with whatever they could get their hands on. Once they'd run out of bricks and bottles to pelt us with, they immediately backed off, unwilling to fight toe to toe. There were similar bouts of violence right up to kick-off. They were playing West Ham and if I was them I would have been relieved to have got inside the ground because we were out for blood that day. We had a brief respite while they watched their team and then we were straight back in.

A few of our boys ended up getting hold of one of their lads and pulling a knife on him. The rest of their firm were pleading with us to let him go: 'Come 'ead la', leave it out, don't slash him,' but if it was one of our lads then they would have cut him to shreds. No doubt about it.

'Help your mate,' I told them.

They carried on begging.

'Help your mate,' I repeated. They obviously hadn't heard me the first time round.

Not one stepped forward.

'Well,' I shrugged, 'He's getting cut then.'

The papers reported that the lad with the knife tried to carve MCFC into the poor cunt's back. He didn't though. He just sliced him up. The Scouser ended up with fifty-one stitches but if you go around slashing people then you can't complain when somebody does the same thing to you. Funnily enough, Andy Nicholls barely mentions this incident in *Scally*, his book about the Everton mob.[12] You would have thought it would be the type of thing he'd have dedicated a couple of paragraphs to. He also said that the Scousers had slashed six City outside Hilton Park service station but if they did it was probably six of our shirters.

Another thing that Andy neglects to mention in his book is the disgraceful attitude of their supporters towards the black members of our firm. Everton came onto the platform at Euston later that day, shouting, 'Get the nigger,' and pointing out the only black lad we had with us to the transport police. They claimed that he was the one who had slashed the lad's back and he ended up getting arrested. They didn't have a single black hooligan with them, which is not surprising because they are one of the most racist firms around. I've got no time for prejudiced people and the Scousers are as bigoted as they come. Manchester is multicultural and well-integrated, whereas Liverpool is mostly white, bar a small West Indian community in Toxteth. Race was never an issue for us but that didn't mean it wasn't an issue for the black lads in our mob. Not everyone was as tolerant as us and in certain areas the colour of a person's skin could mean the difference between going home in a taxi and going home in the back of a police car.

The race issue aside, one of the reasons there was so much animosity was that we were pretty similar. The Cockneys would mistake us for the Mickeys whenever we went down south, as we dressed the same and got up to the same things. They were into robbing fruit machines, just like we were, and they travelled in similar sorts of numbers. We'd wind them up by singing songs about how they'd never get a job and they'd level a similar set of songs straight back at us. Our songs were better though and my favourite was 'In Your Liverpool Slums', which takes the piss out of the hovels they live in.

The battles we waged were psychological as well as physical. It was about getting under their skin. Sometimes we'd catch one of their lads and pretend that we were going to cut him, just to watch him shit himself. You've got to remember this is the same firm that slashed a

---

[12] The book was published in 2002.

Middlesbrough scarfer in the eye while he was walking his son to the car. So they deserved whatever came their way. They may have looked like us and acted like us but the subtle differences between us were enough to fuel mutual hatred.

Every now and again, we'd stumble across a lone Scouser strimming the machines at the arcade. We'd form a circle around him and tell him he was going to get done. Sometimes he'd be pleading with us not to cut him. I was the peacemaker. I'd tell the rest of the firm not to take liberties. You can't pick the stragglers off; it's not in the spirit of things.

To their credit, some of the Scousers had the same mentality. I was busy playing the machines when a big mob of Mickeys caught me unawares. They crowded round me and told me that I was going to get a blade in me. Luckily, one of their lot pushed his way to the front and ushered me outside before they had a chance to carry out the threat.

'Look, just fuck off. Save your skin. If you wait around here you're going to get fucking murdered.'

Fair plays to the fella, he was doing me a favour. But I wasn't having any of it.

'I'm going nowhere,' I told him. 'I'm waiting for my mates to get here and then we'll see.'

I knew the rest of the Guvnors were due at any minute.

'It doesn't have to be like this,' the Scouser told me. 'Get on your way, lad.'

His name was Paul and he didn't see the point in thirty lads ganging up on a single opponent. If it wasn't for him I would have been cut to shreds, which just goes to show that every firm has its good Samaritans as well as its villains. Sometimes it's more rewarding to do the right thing than it is to do a rival lad.

We've had a few close shaves with the Mickeys. Our game against Everton at Goodison Park in the quarter final of the FA cup in 1980/81 was one of the scariest matches I've ever been to. It was a night game and we drew two all. City were losing all the way through and then Paul Power scored an equaliser in the final few minutes. We were made up. We'd salvaged an unlikely draw, which made them fucking furious. The minute I got outside the ground, a load of their lads came rushing out of the bushes, armed with sticks and Stanley knives. Before I got a chance to take it in, the geezer standing next to me had been whacked in the nose and the bloke in front of me had been slashed across the face.

I was only young and there were hundreds of the fuckers. None of the buses had a single window left by the time we arrived back at Lime Street. They looked like a bomb had hit them. Some of the lads were ripping the seats out and throwing them at the Mickeys and some of them were trying to get off the bus to get at them but, being honest, they would have been torn limb from limb if they'd got out. The Scousers were looking to kill somebody that night. A couple of City fans got slashed and there were countless other injuries. It was one of the first genuinely naughty matches I'd been to and it showed what could happen when things got out of hand.

We came unstuck a couple of times at Goodison Park. When I went there again on 2 May 1987, I knew what to expect and yet the Scousers still came out on top. A sixty-strong mob of City got off the train at Lime Street and headed up the road to Las Vegas, one of the arcades frequented by Everton's mob. As we drew near to the arcade, we were confronted by a horde of knife-wielding Mickeys, intent on causing us some serious damage. There were four slashings within the first five minutes and it was all City lads. Two got it in the face and the other two had their arms cut up. Just as we were starting to get the upper hand, the Old Bill turned up and escorted us to the ground. I didn't know it at the time but the Mickeys had an undercover copper with them and he must have alerted his colleagues to what was going on.

As we were making our way to the game, one of the Scousers pulled an air rifle out and shot one of our lads in the chin. The pellet lodged in his flesh and he wasn't allowed to break the escort to get it out. 'You step off this pavement and you're nicked,' a copper told him. He had a fucking bullet stuck in his chin! The Merseyside Old Bill are some of the worst police in the country and that's no word of a lie. They're horrible bastards. They knew full well our pal was injured but they couldn't have cared less.

By the time we got to the ground, we were pissed off with the Mickeys. Not only had they done us over at Vegas but they'd also managed to embed a piece of metal in a lad's chin while he was sur-rounded by Old Bill. We had a top mob with us and if you watch the footage of the game, you'll see part of the City end emptying twenty minutes before the final whistle. That was us heading out to look for their lads. They were nowhere to be seen. They knew that what they'd done at the arcades had been naughty and they were scared of what we might do.

They were a nasty little mob the Mickeys. They loved their weapons and they didn't fight fair but, then again, who defines what's fair and what isn't? Each firm has its own code of conduct. It would be easy to say they've brought football hooliganism into disrepute with the knives thing but you can't dismiss their entire mob based on the actions of a couple of idiots. There's good and bad in every firm.

Now that I'd been to a couple of naughty matches, I was less fazed by the regular, non-tooled up mobs we came across. When you've seen somebody getting slashed up, a couple of punches are nothing by comparison. The levels of violence I was experiencing were gradually increasing. I was getting myself into more and more extreme situations and I was thriving on the danger. I never got the chance to go rock climbing or bungee jumping so fighting with groups of rival supporters was my extreme sport. I was an adrenaline junkie, addicted to risk.

And now that Everton had upped the stakes by using weapons, I was gambling with my life.

9

COVENTRY

People like to say that hooligans aren't real supporters and fair dos, some of them might not be, but when it came to the Guvnors, we were as real as they came. We were working-class lads but we'd go to every match, home or away, whether we had the money or not. If we didn't have the cash to buy a rail ticket, there were a number of different ways of getting there free of charge. Where there's a will there's a way and if you're a dedicated hooligan, you will do what it takes to get your fix. Where City went, I followed. Where the Guvnors went trouble was never far behind.

Coventry on the other hand were a classic example of a firm that didn't travel. It was a pity because they would have got a lot of respect if they had ventured outside their home city. Remember that Specials song 'Ghost Town'? Well the Specials were from Coventry and the lyrics sum the place up to a tee. It's full of abandoned buildings and derelict nightclubs. When we first went there, I would say that it was one of the roughest places in England, although it didn't have the outward appearance of a tough city. Manchester is full of empty warehouses and imposing industrial chimneys, whereas Coventry is deceptively spacious and a lot less claustrophobic than you'd expect from a city of its size. Still, appearances can be deceptive because it was a dangerous place.

Luckily for us, we had a secret weapon in the form of our very own Coventry blue. We'd nicknamed him 'Coventry' for want of a better name and he had picked up a fair bit of information about their firm. He knew what pubs they drank in, what type of numbers they pulled and what time they set off to the match. He was a decent lad, although he was the spitting image of Joe 90[13] and in many ways clueless. We were always filling his head with rubbish. We told him that one of the lads was going out with a bird with no legs and then we fed him stories about how he'd hang her up by her arms so that he could give her one.

'Does he mind people talking about it?' he asked.

This was our cue to wind him up some more.

'Don't mention it in front of him,' I warned. 'You don't know him well enough to be talking about his missus like that.'

I could barely contain my laughter.

'I've never seen him with anyone in a wheelchair,' he mused.

'Oh he doesn't bother with a wheelchair. Can you imagine him pushing one of those things around? Nah, he just puts her under his arm and carries her around. She's only three foot tall now that her legs have gone,' I told him.

From that moment on, he was always proper awkward around the lad that we were talking about. We'd try to slip in little references here and there, like 'Are you getting legless this weekend?' and 'I heard he didn't have a leg to stand on.' He must have thought we were a right bunch of bastards.

Clueless as he was, Coventry was City through and through. He wasn't from Manchester but, as far as I was concerned, he was an honorary Mancunian. He was there when you needed him and that was all that mattered.

It took us an hour and a half to get to Coventry (the place) when we played them in August 1985. It was the first game of the season and we spent the journey down there trading war stories and discussing tactics. It was a hot summer's day and we were boiling our arses off the whole way. We pulled into the station at midday and the minute we set foot outside, they were on us.

Coventry's mob was known as The Legion and contained a mix of young lads and burly, fully-grown men. Some firms were all young kids while others would be all middle-aged blokes. We pelted them with missiles and they hung back, apprehensive about walking into a hail of bricks and broken bottles.

---

[13] A 1960s television series featuring a schoolboy who led a double life as a spy.

I was wearing a bright orange jumper. I couldn't have picked a more conspicuous choice of clothing if I'd tried. It was an error on my part. I stood out like a set of neon lights.

'Oi, you there.'

It was the Old Bill. If there were any witnesses, I wouldn't be difficult for them to identify. All they'd have to say was: 'It was the guy in the orange top,' and I'd be fucked.

'What do you want?' I asked the dibble, acting like an innocent bystander. He was standing next to an anxious-looking shopkeeper.

'Is this the fella who smashed your window?' the copper asked.

To be honest, I can't remember if I smashed it or not. I could have done but I probably didn't.

'I don't know. It's hard to say really,' she whimpered.

I was wearing a luminous orange jumper for Christ's sake. I could see the Old Bill standing there thinking, 'Okay, it couldn't have been him because she would have remembered somebody wearing a daft top like that.'

'Sorry to trouble you,' he said, an air of disappointment in his voice. 'There's been a bit of trouble here, you see. I thought you might have been involved.'

As soon as the copper had fucked off, I was back on the scene, hurling whatever I could get my hands on at Coventry's mob. After a brief standoff, we rallied our troops and charged, kicking and punching them as they struggled to stand their ground. I could see worried faces in their ranks. All that was needed was a little more pressure and they would come unstuck.

Hooligans are like dominoes. The moment one falls, the rest follow suit. After a few minutes of going at it with them, they lost their nerve and backed off into a nearby subway. We surged forwards, capitalising on their fading morale. A couple of backwards paces rapidly transformed into a full-scale retreat. They were on the run. It was a good thing we'd turned out in force or we would have been hammered. We had a brief stop to catch our breath and then continued on our way through the city centre towards their stadium, Highfield Road.

The game itself was a 1–1 draw, which was actually a result for us, as they had an excellent team that season while we were, yet again, to finish in the bottom half of the table. Coventry's ground is fucking miles away from the station. If we'd have had the full firm with us then we would have relished the chance to have another run-in with their lads. As it was, we managed to get separated from the rest of our mob. There were only twelve of us left and we were pretty fucking vulnerable. There was me, Farmer, Patty, Michael Ossie, Frankie, Coventry and a couple of others. Despite us having Coventry[14] on board, we still managed to get ourselves hopelessly lost almost as soon as we came out of the ground. Coventry[15] were everywhere. We could hear them discussing in which direction we had headed and searching around the streets for us.

After an eternity traipsing around the same housing estate trying to find our way out, one of Coventry's lads had the bright idea to run us over. I've heard of people coming to matches tooled up but I think it's fair to say that driving into someone in a car isn't really what hooliganism is about. Noticing that the driver was clutching a metal baseball bat, I grabbed hold of a milk bottle and smashed it against the wall, ready to stab him with the jagged edge. At the same time Farmer took his belt off so that he could whip him with it. By this stage, a group of Coventry had piled out of the car and were rapidly advancing, bats in hands.

'Come any closer and I'll stick this in your ugly fucking faces,' I warned, brandishing the broken bottle.

They obviously thought I was bluffing because they came up close. But we don't fuck about. If we say we're going to do something then 99 per cent of the time we will. The next thing they knew, one of them had got a bottle cracked over his head and they were piling back into their car. I thought, 'There you go, have that you bastard.' It was him or me and I was relieved it ended up being him.

There must have been fifty Coventry scattered through the estate. We could hear footsteps and screeching tyres as some of them searched for us in cars while the rest pursued us on foot. We were climbing over fences and running through people's gardens in a desperate attempt to get away and it was getting to the point where they had us surrounded.

---

[14] The lad, not the firm
[15] The firm, not the lad

'Arm yourselves lads,' I told the rest of the boys.

If it came on top we would need weapons, however makeshift, to give us a fighting chance. We ripped up a fencepost and picked up the pieces, ready to crack some skulls.

So there we were, wandering around the streets armed with big wooden sticks, preparing for war. It would have been a lot easier if we hadn't have got ourselves separated from the rest of the lads. This was in the days before mobile phones. If you got split up, there was no way of finding out where the rest of the firm were. Luckily for us, we eventually stumbled across a signpost, pointing us in the direction of the station. It was five minutes up the road and I could see a group of our lads waiting at the entrance. We'd made it back in one piece, or so we thought.

Just as we were mopping the sweat from our brows and breathing a sigh of relief, a carload of Coventry came skidding around the corner and a load of their lads jumped out. It was time to smash their car up. I hurled a brick through the windscreen and the rest of the boys launched whatever they could get their hands on at the driver and his pals.

'My car!' he yelled, as if it was somehow out of order for us to be putting his windows in.

'Well you didn't seem that bothered about it when you were trying to run us over,' I replied.

And it was true. You can't complain about somebody vandalising your car when you've been skidding around like a lunatic, attempting to mow people down.

After a brief exchange of blows, Coventry's mob retreated back to the estate and we continued on our way up the road. They had turned out in force for us and if they travelled in the types of numbers that they pulled at home games they'd have been a force to reckon with. It had been a close shave and that's what made it such an exciting afternoon. Most people would have been terrified at the prospect of being surrounded by bat-wielding hooligans but I found it exhilarating. We could have been beaten to a bloody pulp but we weren't. We'd made our way through enemy territory and come out the other side in one piece.

Part of the thrill of going to an away game was the challenge of navigating an unknown and hostile city and living to tell the tale. It was a chance for us to take another team's firm on in their own back-yard. Above all, it was an excuse to get together, see a bit of the country and show the locals what we were made of. We weren't the type of lads who would sit about waiting for the action to come to us.

We were invaders as well as defenders and Coventry was another conquered city to add to the collection.

10

PREPARE FOR THE WORST

We expected a strong turnout from Coventry, but there were games where firms attached to smaller clubs took us by surprise. Every now and then, we would come up against a mob that we'd severely under-estimated. We assumed that we could stroll into their hometown and walk out again without a scratch.

Reading isn't a town you would think has much of a mob. Manchester is a rough city. Travel into the city centre from either direction and you'll see looming tower blocks, silhouetted against the skyline. Make the same journey into Reading and you'll see historic buildings and middle-class commuters hopping onto the London train. I have to admit that I thought very little about going up against them when we played them on 14 November 1987. In my mind it was just another game in which City were going to be beaten. We were both in the old second division (then the second tier of English football) and Reading didn't have much of a reputation to maintain.

The plan was to watch the game and then go up to London to look for the Yids. We were excited about having it with Spurs but we didn't give Reading a second thought. Don't get me wrong, we were always prepared for trouble but we didn't think they'd have many in their firm or be well organised. We only had twenty lads with us. There was me, Frankie, Little Spinner, a few of the other usual faces and Larry and E.T. from London.

As soon as we got off the train, we made our way to the ground so that the Old Bill didn't get onto us. People like to stereotype hooligans as drunken idiots who sit about in the pub for hours but that couldn't be further from the truth. Most of the lads stay off the beer because it's best to have your wits about you on match days. It's also easy to be picked off in small groups if you're all in different pubs.

When we got to the ground, we did our usual trick of jumping the turnstiles, although we had to go in the home end because there were coppers at ours checking tickets and searching fans. There was one guy on the stiles at the Reading end. If he ran after us then everybody who was behind us would go in without paying. I had no intention of forking out what little money I had to watch a team that was originally created for the benefit of the poor. Football is all about money but I'm glad to say I've never contributed a penny, choosing instead to pay for my entertainment in blood, sweat and tears by fighting for City.

The game itself was uneventful, although I seem to recall us winning 2–0. There was no smoking in the seating area and a pair of Old Bill came over to harass us, saying that we were lighting fags up. I was just about to tell them to fuck off when the Reading fans we were sitting next to vouched for us and told them that we weren't doing anything wrong. The tabloids are always running stories saying how we terrorise ordinary fans but we were sat in the midst of opposition scarfers and there they were sticking up for us.

We left the game early to try and get back to the station before the police. Reading's firm were the last thing on my mind. I was preoccupied thinking about Tottenham. There was a big crowd of Reading fans leaving at the same time as us so we blended in with them. If we were the hooligans you read about in *The Sun* and the *Daily Mirror* then we would have done them but the fact is that we don't take liberties. The amount of times when we've actually saved the shirt wearers from other mobs is ridiculous but do they thank us for it? Like fuck they do. Hooligans are what the Mods and Rockers were in the Sixties. The media blame us whenever someone gets hurt.

As we got further away from the stadium, the Reading fans began to trail off in different directions until it was just us left. We'd been anonymous in the crowd but, now that it had dispersed, we were starting to get some funny looks. One lad in particular was giving us the eye, a cocky, half-caste kid. He was definitely following us as well.

'What the fuck are you doing following us?' one of our lads

demanded. 'If you want a row then fuck off and come back with your boys.'

I was beginning to sense that they were more of a threat than I had originally anticipated. Every team has a firm but I'd always thought that a little club like Reading would have a few random thugs who didn't know what they were doing. Five minutes further down the road, they taught me a valuable lesson: never underestimate your opponent.

'Ere lads, what's this?' yelled one of our frontrunners.

Sure enough, there was a big mob of Reading, tearing down the street. There were fifty of the cunts, double the number we had. At first we hung back, shocked at what a good turnout they had. Then, when the adrenaline kicked in, we charged forward, ready to show them that, although they had superior manpower, we were undaunted.

Soon after it kicked off another little mob turned up, with the half-caste lad leading the way. By this stage, we were on the back foot and slowly beginning to lose it. I was fighting with one of their lads when I noticed that everyone else was making a run for it. I turned round to follow them but, as I was getting away, somebody grabbed me and slammed me into a shop window. Luckily for me the glass didn't give but while I was struggling to remain upright, I noticed one of their lot opening up a butterfly knife.

Just as the geezer was coming across to cut me, I heard Errol, one of our black lads, shouting, 'They've got Benny. Turn around.'

But before the rest of the firm had a chance to follow his instructions, he had run over and kicked the knife out of the Reading lad's hand. Errol is Rodney Rhoden's brother, another of our top boys, and someone you might know from his book *The Young Guvnors*.[16] Like his brother he is a handy lad and you can't fault his loyalty. If he hadn't come back for me I would have been cut to ribbons. The minute he jumped in, I managed to break one of my hands free and I started punching and kicking anything that moved. By this stage, the rest of the mob had got it together and were piling in. Reading must have been surprised that we were coming back for more because they started to back off.

---

[16] The book was published in 2008.

Now that they were on the run, we decided that it would be a good time to get on our train, as we needed to get to the station before the police showed up. We were striding proudly down the street, buzzing at how we had managed to turn things round, when we heard a southern voice yell: 'Come on, you Manc bastards.'

These cunts were insatiable!

There were even more of them this time, at least a hundred. A couple of them had carrier bags full of bricks and they started throwing them. It was like being in a meteor shower. We managed to get to the station entrance and then we thought: 'Let them come to us. There's no point walking through a big shower of missiles to get at them.'

By this stage, the transport police had noticed that something was amiss. A female copper came out of the station to see what the noise was about and got a half-brick bounced off her forehead. She slumped to the floor, oozing claret all over the pavement. Now I hate the police more than anyone but it isn't nice to see a woman covered in her own blood. 'She's going to die. Let's get her into the station,' I said to Errol.

Errol, me and another lad dragged the copper to safety, feeling her warm, wet blood against our clothing as we set her down behind the doors. If we'd left her there, she could easily have been killed by Reading but that's one they'd never print in *The Sun*: 'Hooligans Save Copper's Life'. It's funny how whenever we do something bad it makes the front page but whenever we help somebody, the story goes untold.

We left the copper at the front of the station and charged back into the mêlée. We were pissed off because they had so many more lads than us but yet still felt the need to arm themselves with bricks. 'Fuck this,' I thought. 'They can arm themselves with a fucking nuclear bomb for all I care. I'm still going to kick the shit out of them.' Bruises heal but pride doesn't and, when it comes down to it, whether it's one on one, or one on a hundred, it's about how much of a fight you put up. There are no winners or losers in football violence. It's about giving as good as you get.

Rather than going tooled up like some other firms, the Guvnors improvised with stones, bottles, chairs and tables. Sometimes we'd even steal umbrellas, using the steel tip as a makeshift bayonet. I was lucky enough to find a large stick. It was time to play them at their own game.

ET was right beside me, whipping fuck out of them with his belt. At this point, their boys realised we weren't backing down and they made a run for it. They were brave when we were unarmed and they had carrier bags full of bricks. Now we were up close and personal, they were a lot less confident.

I was thinking, 'Fuck me; that better be the last of them this time. We've got a train to catch and we're going to be here all day at this rate.' We were walking into the station when a load of Old Bill rushed over and started their usual bullyboy games.

'We've seen what you've been up to,' they told us, as they pushed us up against the wall. Well if that was true I had one question for them: why did they stand there and let their colleague get pelted with bricks?

Luckily, the woman dibble was up off her arse by this point.

'What are you doing?' she interjected. 'You can't arrest them. They saved me and they were only defending themselves.'

Her white shirt was soaking with blood, as if someone had thrown a bucket of red paint over her. The coppers looked dejected. It was obvious she was telling the truth. There was debris littering the streets and it didn't take a rocket scientist to figure out what had happened to her.

As I say, I normally haven't got much time for the police but this lady copper was all right and if it wasn't for her we would have been nicked for violent disorder. As it was, her so-called colleagues slunk off to their unmarked car, tails firmly between their legs. We had done their job for them. They should have been on hand to protect her but they were too busy looking for reasons to arrest us. So much for their morals; I would never have left a mate to get done in like that. But I guess coppers are people just like us. You get good ones like the lady copper and bad ones like the rest of them.

By this stage, the London train was at the platform and I thought we were going to miss it. The police were at the barriers checking tickets and there was no way of sneaking through. One of the boys turned to the female cop and asked her if there was any chance that she could get us onto the platform because our train was there and we didn't want to miss it.

'Of course,' she told us. 'Just run through.'

Predictably, the other coppers were having none of it.

'It's all right, they've got tickets,' she assured them.

She was telling the truth. It was just that they were return tickets from Manchester to Reading. We just made it onto the train as the doors were closing. What a day. We'd been surprised when sixty Reading turned up so imagine what a head fuck it was when a hundred of them showed up later on. I've heard that Reading have a decent firm nowadays and I'd like to think we showed them how it's done, although from the looks of things they had a pretty good idea already.

As soon as we got to London, the Yids were waiting. A lad got slashed and I got hit in the face with nunchucks. We knew it was going to kick off there and that's what we went down for. Tottenham, like City, are a big club with a big firm, whereas Reading are one of those teams that usually finds itself in the lower leagues.

* * *

There were a few games like that where we were been taken by surprise. Southend was another. It was a poxy midweek League Cup fixture in September 1986 and I didn't expect much to go off. What I didn't count on was our old friends the Yids turning up.

I hate Southend. It's a third-rate Morecambe, which is a third-rate Blackpool. If it wasn't for the old East Enders taking nostalgic day trips there the government would be best advised to cover the place with sand and erase its name from the atlas. Whenever we go down south, we always go via London, as it gives Tottenham a chance to meet us. We're usually fairly well-behaved on the trains although we try to scam the ticket inspector and a few of us like to have a drink and a few spliffs. Apart from that, we just sit there chatting. Speed is my drug of choice and I was speeding the whole way down. It gets your adrenaline pumping and it hypes you up for a row. It's not a good idea to drink or smoke if you're taking whiz so I mainly stuck to the phet.

When we got to Euston, we were met by a couple of Gooners, who told us that Spurs were planning on ambushing us at Southend. We've always had a good relationship with the Gooners and there have been a few times when they've fought side by side with us against Tottenham. We thanked them for the tip and hopped on the train to

Southend. Not having factored in a clash with the Yids, there were only twenty-five of us. You set off expecting a quiet day and end up coming up against one of your biggest rivals!

We arrived at the station around five and, fuck me, Southend was shit. No wonder the crime rate and the birth rate are both high there because there's fuck all else to do. They were filming an episode of *EastEnders* in the town centre so we did our best to put a stop to that. It was pissing it down with rain and they wanted to shoot the scene as quickly as possible but we were in the background the whole time, singing City songs and trying to put them off. It kept us amused for a few hours before the match and it was an extra challenge for the programme makers. Anyway, it's called *EastEnders* so they should have been filming it in the East End and not on the south coast.

When we got to the ground, our first priority was to blag our way in. There are certain grounds where you can't easily jump the turnstiles so I went over to the ticket office to clock the names on the list of complimentary tickets. While I was busy trying to work out who we could pretend to be in order to blag our way into the ground, a mob of seventy Yids appeared behind us. It was an ambush. They had their hands in their pockets as well, a sign that blades are going to be coming out. There were only eight of us, the rest of the firm were God-knows-where. There was Frankie, this big lad Lee Skelly from Wythenshawe and a couple of others from round them sides. They were all good boys but there's only so much that eight can do against seventy.

The Yids formed a semi-circle around us, trying to intimidate us. I was focussing on their faces, taking in as much detail as I could so that I would recognise them when I next saw them. I would have my revenge.

'Shall I cut him?' one of their lads asked, taking a blade from his pocket.

'You're taking liberties again. You've all got tools and there are eight of us,' I warned him.

I half expected him to slash me right there and then.

'Okay Benny, remember this,' he replied. 'We don't take liberties.'

And with that, they walked away. We were double lucky. I know we would have had it with them, as the lads that I was with were game as fuck, but we would have suffered some serious damage in the process.

Wiping the sweat from our brows, we hurried off to find the rest of the firm before we got into any more trouble. The match itself was fucking boring, a nil, nil draw. Typical City, we never win at home and we never win away. We left at the final whistle and somehow managed to make it back to the station before anything kicked off. When it did finally go off, we could see Tottenham coming towards us but it didn't immediately register. Then, before my brain caught up with my eyes, they were on us.

First came the gas. CS gas is horrible stuff. Not only does it sting like fuck but also you can't tell what the hell's going on. While we were stumbling around, struggling to see what we were up against, a load of Yids were piling into us, twatting us all over the shop with sticks. There were two sets of Yids: the London Yids and a separate firm from Basildon, who had joined up with them. We retreated, taken aback at the amount that had turned up. As soon as we caught our breath and wiped the water from our eyes, we were straight back into the fray, picking up whatever we could find to throw at them.

I was in the thick of it fighting for my life when I felt a heavy blow on the side of my arm. Some cunt had hit me with an iron bar. I was in the middle of the road and all I could think was that I had to stay upright or I would get run over. Thwack! He struck me again with it, this time across the back. 'Fuck me,' I thought. 'If I get hit by a car I'm going to be in a bad way.' Frankie was getting it just as bad. He was being twatted in the face. The situation really wasn't looking too good.

I managed to stay on my feet long enough to grab a brick and bounce it off some poor bloke's head. I was just starting to get the upper hand when one of their lads booted me hard between the legs. I'm not going to lie, it was fucking painful. I doubled over, holding my balls and groaning. When the pain had finally gone, I looked up and, to my surprise, the fighting had stopped. They'd timed it so that they could hit us and then be back on the next train to London. You've got to hand it to them. They played a blinder that day. It was a perfectly orchestrated attack. There was a short, sharp burst of violence and then they were off before the police turned up.

We had done well to get away with just a couple of cuts and bruises. Skelly had a broken ankle but no-one was seriously injured. You go to

Southend and you expect shit weather and depressing scenery but you don't expect two mobs of Yids to join forces and kick the living fuck out of you. But, then again, when you're a Young Guvnor trouble finds you and when it doesn't you go looking for it.

When you're involved in football violence, it pays to have your wits about you. Obviously, you can't be on your guard the whole time but if you're with City there's always the chance of a row. Tottenham could have sliced me up that day, so respect to them for leaving it until I had a few more boys with me. When you live the type of life that I do, there's no such thing as a trouble-free game. And anyway, it's the last thing on earth you would want.

* * *

Sometimes we'd travel to a city with the express purpose of having a row and there'd be no-one there to fight. I remember when we were due to play Luton on 30 November 1985. It was after we'd managed to work our way back up to the first division and we stopped off in the capital on the way, hoping to have a ruck with Everton. They were playing one of the London teams and we had our fingers crossed that we'd bump into them at the station. We didn't bank on getting hassle from Luton. We classed them as similar to Watford, whose firm are a fucking joke. Besides, the Luton fans had been pelted with bricks outside Maine Road when they relegated us in 1982/83 and it was hard to picture them as a threat after that. They'd run back into their section of the ground and refused to come back out, hardly a mental image designed to have us quaking in our boots.

We missed Everton. It was disappointing but there was still a faint chance that Luton would turn out. You never know what a team's firm is capable of until you've been up against them so we could never rule out anyone. Luton weren't in the same league as Tottenham or Chelsea but we'd heard that they'd had a row with QPR earlier in the season. Saying that, we knew fuck all about QPR and for all we knew they could have been a firm full of nobodies.

I was always buzzing when the train pulled into the station at the final destination. I'd be looking out the windows to see if I could catch sight of any floodlights and trying to work out in which direction the ground lay. The station is quite small so I got the impression that Luton itself isn't all that big. You can tell a lot about a town by the size of its station. If it's a massive building with a lot of platforms then it's usually in a decent-sized city, whereas if it's a pokey little thing with a few trains crammed in then it's either somewhere small or there's nothing worth travelling there for.

Hooliganism provided me with the chance to trek around the country and explore different towns and cities. I wouldn't have bothered going to half of the places if it wasn't for the football. I remember hearing people saying 'I've never been to London. I've always wanted to go there,' and thinking, 'Hold on a minute, you've never been to London? What's wrong with you?' By the time I was in my early twenties, I'd been all over England, thanks to the Guvnors.

Travelling to a match was an excuse to get away from it all. We'd go to a place that we knew fuck all about and walk around the city centre as if we owned it. It was the ultimate bonding experience and when there are forty of you wandering around a strange and potentially hostile city the camaraderie is out of this world. We were like Vikings, trekking to a foreign land and leaving a path of destruction in our wake. Richard Branson can afford to travel round the world in a balloon but when you're from a working-class background, you have to find your adventures in less conventional places.

We had some handy lads with us. Anthony Rowan was there and he was one of the most fearless people you will ever meet. I remember when Fulham came to City, trying to throw their weight around. He was walking down Portland Street when fifty of them came striding down the road.

'We're fackin' Fulham,' they told him, giving it all that.

'I don't give a fuck who you are,' he sneered.

It wasn't one of those situations where he knew that he could kick it off because there was a load of City round the corner. He was properly on his own but he didn't give a fuck. He took them all on and although he came out of it in a worse state than them, you've got to hand it to him for standing his ground and refusing to back down. It's sad though. Anthony now has multiple sclerosis and is virtually paralysed. He went

A bit of nostalgia.

Bez bleeding outside the Clarence after a game with United.

On the move again.

Some of our black lads.

The Guvnors on the move.

The horses arrive.

The lads.

The lads at a game.

The legend that is daft Donald.

The Guvnors, portrait of a mob.

I was born and raised in Gorton and I still consider it my spiritual home. This photo shows me in front of a typical street scene in Gorton, characterised by rows of terraced housing.

'Gangs bent on violence'

UNDERCOVER detectives infiltrated a gang of football hooligans whose purpose was to "attack intimidate and terrorise" supporters of opposing teams, a jury was told today.

Liverpool Crown Court heard the gang was made up of two groups called the Governors and the Young Governors who followed Manchester City games.

Five Manchester men, aged 18 to 26, deny a number of charges including conspiracy to riot.

Their arrest followed Operation Omega launched by the police at the start of the 1987-88 season involving undercover officers.

The two groups, aged from their mid-teens to late twenties, had a "hard core" of about 30 members, said Mr David Sumner, prosecuting.

He said the Governors' purpose was not to support Manchester City — "their interest in some cases did not extend to football at all — but on violence for its own sake.

For home games, members would go to City's Maine Road ground but never enter the game to avoid detection by security cameras.

Before the court, accused of conspiring to riot and conspiring to cause violent disorder, were Adrian Gunning, aged 18, of Bletchley Close, Longsight; David Foulkes, a labourer, aged 25, of Clinton Avenue, Fallowfield; Andrew Bennion, aged 21, of Solway Road, Wythenshawe; Ian Valentine, aged 18, a probation officer, of Green End, Hamilton Green, Denton, and David Goodall, aged 23, a warehouse man, of Beckton Gardens, Benchill, Wythenshawe.

Mr Foulkes denies three other charges of riot and Mr Goodall pleads not guilty to two other riot accusations.

Earlier, 21 men admitted conspiring to cause violent disorder. Sentence was deferred until June 5.

All were found not guilty of conspiring to riot.

(Proceeding).

How Guvnors were smashed
Omega was best operation ever
News Focus by PAUL HORROCKS

Policeman in soccer gang was forced to quit

By Paul Horrocks

AN UNDERCOVER detective who infiltrated a gang of soccer hooligans suffered a breakdown because of the fear of being exposed, a court heard today.

He spent several weeks posing as a soccer thug attached to two gangs of Manchester City louts known as the Guvnors and the Young Guvnors.

Twenty-five hooligans were appearing at Liverpool Crown Court for sentence after admitting conspiring to cause violent disorder.

Mr David Sumner, prosecuting, said that in August, 1987, undercover officers infiltrated and monitored the activities of the gangs.

They showed a remarkable degree of courage" and "witnessed appalling violence, but were unable to intervene.

Mr Sumner revealed that after several weeks the masquerade was too much for one officer and he had a breakdown.

One hooligan, Vincent George, 17, of Wythenshawe Road, Brooklands, Sale kept "match reports" of violence. His detailed diary, entitled War Games, was read in court.

It described the violence in Manchester city centre, as a group of Oldham fans arrived to watch a match at Maine Road.

The Operation Omega trial, held in Liverpool in 1989, was heavily covered by the media and ended with most of us getting prison sentence and football-banning orders.

Mickey Francis, a prominent Guvnor and like me the author of a book on his experience.

This is me outside Liverpool Crown Court with one of my co-accused.

The Old Bill always kept a close eye on us.

The paparazzi – it sounds funny but the constant surveillance paid off for the dibble during Operation Omega.

Watching us watching you.

from being a fit, healthy lad to suffering from a crippling, incurable disease. Despite that he's a Guvnor through and through and the reputation he built up all those years ago can never be taken from him, regardless of how bad his illness gets.

There were a couple of other game lads with us: Frankie, Luke, Tony and a few of the other familiar faces and, as the train doors opened, the hairs on my arms were tingling. This was it. We would either have it with Luton or return home disappointed. The ball was in their court.

Luton town centre looked like a right fucking toy town. It reminded me of Broughton precinct[17] and you couldn't shoplift there either, so we decided to make our way to Kenilworth Road. As we approached the ground, we were confronted by the sight of fifty Luton, trying their hardest to barge their way into the ticket office. A couple of our older lads had barricaded themselves in and Luton were determined to get at them. They were in high spirits, chanting:

'Who sent Man City down? Luton Town, Luton Town.'

Yeah, fair enough, but who got bricked outside the ground and ran back inside to hide? Here's a clue: it wasn't City.

As we drew closer, one of their lads clocked us and started shouting, 'We're M.I.G.s. Come on, you Northern cunts.'

M.I.G. stands for Men In Gear and it's the name of Luton's main firm. They set off to meet us but we had a tactical advantage, as we were heading downhill and they had to hike up a steep slope. Most of our lads were in their late teens, whereas the majority of their mob were in their mid twenties. We were younger and fitter than they were. We charged in, kicking and punching until they backed off, unable to keep their composure in the face of forty snarling Guvnors baying for blood. One of them had the bright idea of trying to run back into the ticket office but Deano, another of our double-game lads, opened the door and promptly weighed him in.

Deano was one of our handiest lads until he had a run-in with a QPR fan and ended up on a life-support machine. He'd been brawling away when one of their lads plunged a knife into his leg, puncturing a

---

[17] Broughton precinct is a rundown shopping centre in inner-city Salford.

major artery. He's never been the same since then. You can say boo to him and he'll jump a mile. He's into his comic books nowadays, Marvel superheroes and all of that. Whatever floats his boat, I guess.

It's not unusual for people who have been badly injured to lose their bottle and decide to pack it in. One of United's older lads got stabbed by one of our lot and ended up doing the same thing. I've had a blade put to me a couple of times and it's never put me off going to matches but, then again, everybody's different.

After a brief exchange of blows, Luton eventually retreated down the hill, shouting 'see you later'. Fair play to them: they were in a whole different league to Watford, they had some game lads and they could definitely have a row. The boys who had been trapped inside the ticket office were relieved we had turned up sooner rather than later, as they would have been in trouble if Luton's mob had managed to get in before we arrived.

I can't remember much about the game and, to be honest, it was secondary to what had gone off beforehand. When you're a kid, you want to know the names of the players and you're proper enthusiastic about everything football-related. Then you get to the stage where you're the same age as the players are and you start to look at things differently. It's hard to get excited about a game that your team is constantly losing, especially when there's an area you can excel in off the pitch. City might not have had the best footballers but it did have the best hooligans. We were the crème de la crème, not because we were particularly hard but because we had a passion for what we did. While the shirt wearers were registering their support by spending their wages on overpriced tickets and expensive merchandise, we were demonstrating that we were willing to fight to uphold the pride of our team.

As soon as the match had finished, Luton were on us like a swarm of locusts. Some of them had knives and Tony got his coat slashed up. It was a brand new Aquascutum and he was pretty pissed off. In those days, some lads would dip their hands into their pockets just as it was going off to make out they were tooled up. Sometimes they were faking it but every now and then they'd pull a Stanley out and take a swipe.

I was never one for using weapons. If there's a game on and you're dressed like a hooligan there's a strong chance you're going to end up getting stopped by the Old Bill. If they catch you with a knife you're looking at jail time. It's an unnecessary risk, especially when you can do just as much damage with a rolled-up newspaper. The Millwall brick is one of the hooligan's most effective weapons: you take a standard British tabloid and roll the pages up as tightly as you can, creating a makeshift cosh. You wouldn't have thought that being hit with paper would do anything worth speaking of but Millwall bricks can inflict serious injuries.

Although I avoided carrying tools, anything that was available to pick up and use as a weapon was fair game. The window of a DIY shop got smashed, enabling our lads to arm themselves with the tools they had on display. M.I.G. had some naughty people with them, the type who would slice you open without a moment's hesitation. They quickly followed suit and picked up whatever they could get their hands on from the shop.

Just as the two mobs were really beginning to get stuck in, the Old Bill turned up in force and hauled a load of us off in handcuffs. Fortunately, none of our lads ended up getting charged but it brought a premature end to our battle with Luton. We waited outside the nick until they had released the last of the Guvnors and then made our way back to the station, still proper buzzing. Luton had a decent mob but I reckon we came out on top. Still, they are badly underrated, especially by the big teams. They definitely held their own and, for a team of their size, they had a pretty hefty firm.

After such an action-packed game, you would have thought that we'd have used the journey back to Manchester as an opportunity to relax. As it was, we were hyped up to fuck and a couple of the lads were starting to get on the nerves of our fellow passengers.

'If you don't stop swearing I'm going to call the police,' the ticket collector warned us.

Yeah, right. We carried on using exactly the same language we'd been using before, assuming that he was trying to scare us.

But sure enough, there was a group of British Transport Police waiting for us at the next stop, just as the inspector had promised. We weren't doing anything wrong; we were effing and blinding a bit but that's bound to happen whenever you've got a large group of lads sitting together. We weren't doing it deliberately to cause offence; we were just excited about our run-in with Luton. However, in saying that, only one of us had a valid ticket and the rest of us were pretending to be under sixteen so that we only had to pay £1 each. Now that we had drawn attention to ourselves, we'd have to think on our feet or we could end up being charged with gaining pecuniary advantage, which basically means attempting to jump the train.

'Where are your tickets then?' the copper asked. 'I bet you haven't got any.'

The lad who had a valid ticket held it out, ready for inspection.

'That's one. What about the rest of you?'

I held my ticket out in front of him.

'Let's have a look.'

Just as he was reaching over to check the precise details of the fare I'd paid, I crammed the ticket into my mouth and began to chew it up. The rest of the firm followed suit.

'Oops, we've eaten them,' I told the Old Bill. He'd seen the tickets from a distance and with a bit of luck he would assume that we'd paid our fares and conclude that we were trying to be awkward fuckers.

'Very funny but you'll be laughing on the other side of your face when you get back to Manchester. There's a hefty fine waiting for you,' he smugly informed us.

The copper had the bright idea of locking us in the parcels coach and standing guard over us with a police dog. This was an open invitation for us to take the piss.

'Do you take that thing round primary schools, asking the kids if they want to see your puppies?' I said.

'You probably put it in a bag, ready to lure them out with it,' one of the other lads chimed in.

By this stage, the Old Bill had turned an unhealthy shade of red. There was another hour and a half of the journey left. He should have let us stay in our seats! How else did he expect us to pass the time?

By the time the train had pulled up into Piccadilly, it was a full hour late and there was an angry mob of passengers congregating on the platform.

'It's you that's delayed their train you know,' the copper told us.

We pulled our coats over our heads so that none of the aggrieved commuters would recognise us. I could see them getting ready to mouth off; they were like a pack of hungry wolves baying for blood. The minute we stepped out of the train and onto the platform, we were met by a large group of Manchester transport police, who ushered us through the hostile crowd towards the BTP building at the front of the station. They asked us a couple of questions and then told us we'd be getting issued with £300-worth of fines. They didn't get a penny out of me though because by the time they'd got round to chasing up the money, I was in jail for something else. When you get sent down, they ask you if you've got any outstanding fines and a lot of the time they end up wiping them out. It's a good way of getting out of paying them because sometimes they'll try to take a fiver a week out of your giro without letting on. If the government calculates that £40 a week (or the equivalent in today's money) is the lowest amount you can survive on then how can they justify leaving you £5 short? It will only make people resort to thieving because they're going to get the extra fiver from somewhere.

Reading, Southend and Luton: three nondescript commuter towns and hardly the type of places you would associate with organised hooliganism. Everywhere has its rough bits though and there's an underbelly of violence in every town and city in England. Even Chester and York have got their own firms and they are proper fucking posh. It shows that you can never be 100 per cent sure of what you're getting into. You can travel to a city thinking that it's going to be a walk in the park only to end up going home with your tail between your legs.

We were always prepared for the worst and that was often what we were faced with. While some of the violence was impossible to predict, there were certain matches where a riot was inevitable and when it came to riotous behaviour there was a Cockney firm right at the top of the list. Their ground was known as The Den and going there was like walking into the lair of a ravenous beast, wearing a coat made of raw meat. You have a fair idea of who I'm talking about, the mob that every self-respecting hooligan dreams of facing.

Millwall: a club that has become synonymous with hooliganism.

11

THE LION'S DEN

There are certain mobs that have a rep to them: United for its numbers, us for the obvious reasons, Everton for using tools. And then there's Millwall, known for being good all-rounders. In May 2002, they managed to injure forty-seven policemen and twenty-four horses after a playoff with Birmingham. The fact that they were able to take an entire station full of coppers down sums them up pretty well, I'd say. They're called the Lions for a reason. When you come up against them, you're venturing into the wilderness, into the territory of a vicious predator. They are the most notorious firm in Britain and every bit as nasty as their reputation suggests.

I was buzzing my tits off when I discovered that we were going up against them in December 1987. It was our chance to test our mettle against some of the most violent hooligans in Britain. We were heading into the lion's den, and we didn't give a fuck. Any fear that we might have felt was quickly converted into excitement and the hairs on my arms tingled in anticipation.

Back in those days, football hooliganism was closely connected with the music scene. Watching live music was the logical progression from watching live football and there were certain bands that we would watch whenever they performed. This was partly because we enjoyed what they did and partly to earn enough money to get us to and from matches. We'd do off a load of T-shirts with the name of the band on the front and sell them outside the venue before and after the gig. Most of the bands weren't bothered. They were loaded and they didn't mind us profiting from their success. It wasn't as if we were taking their livelihood away. We were catering for the fans who didn't care if they were buying the real deal. When you're low on money, you aren't as fussed about having something that's legit. Buying snide goods was an opportunity for the poorer attendees to have the things that would have been off limits to them if it wasn't for us being there.

We were doing the in-out at a Happy Mondays concert at the International in Longsight the night before we were due to set off to Millwall. I was pretty chummy with Shaun Ryder, the lead singer, mainly through bumping into him in the city centre. I'm a sociable person, never one to shy away from a conversation. Some people are wary of famous people but although he was a well-known singer I was a well-known hooligan. He had a talent but so did I. It just so happened that I'd opted for something less commercially viable. I was never going to be on daytime television for being a Young Guvnor, whereas he was doing something that appealed to the masses. Hooliganism isn't everybody's cup of tea but everyone likes music and fair play to Shaun for making something of himself. He wasn't one of those celebrities who are up their own arses. He was proper down to earth. You could talk to him exactly how you'd talk to anyone else. It was just unfortunate that he happened to support United!

Shaun was into his drugs and he was proper buzzing about this new set of pills he'd come across in America.

'It was ecstasy,' he told me.

I remember thinking: 'Hold on a minute. I'm a fan of your music but you're blowing your own trumpet a bit there, aren't you mate?'

'Not the music, the pills. They were £25 a pop but, I'll tell you what, I've never had anything like them,' he explained.

Meanwhile, another of our lads was busy selling Bez some draw. You would have thought that he'd have had enough drug dealers hanging around him, given that he was famous for dancing about like he was off his head on acid.

We left the venue at two and headed for the train. I was speeding at the time so I was still full of energy. We walked from Plymouth Grove in Longsight all the way to Stockport station, as we knew the police would be waiting for us at Piccadilly. We always had to be one step ahead of the Old Bill: sometimes we'd arrive at a city three hours before a game was due to start, just to confuse them. It was a battle of wits.

There were a couple of other lads waiting at the station, some were from Stockport, a few were from Wythenshawe and then there was this young lad Dennis who was even smaller than me but fucking game. We were still short on numbers but it would have to do.

We caught the 6.20 to Euston and spent the journey discussing whether Millwall would live up to our expectations. To understand why their mob is such a magnet for hooligans, you have to look at Bermondsey, where they draw their support from. It's one of the most deprived areas in the country and there's little wonder the locals resort to violence, what with them living in a pocket of poverty in an otherwise affluent city. In the wealthier areas of the capital, the residents can do what they want, whereas in the impoverished estates of southeast London, people rely on the cheapest forms of entertainment. Hooliganism is their escape from monotony, their way of elevating themselves above the dilapidated surroundings. Millwall isn't the most glamorous club but it has one of the most active sets of hooligans. For some that is a reason to despair; for others, it's a source of pride.

When we arrived at Euston, there were another twenty City lads waiting. Most were from Levenshulme, just south of Gorton, and they were all real front-liners. I was relieved to see them. We would have been badly outnumbered otherwise. Now that we were sixty-strong, we decided to walk to London Bridge and plot up there for a while. We found a half-decent pub and the rest of the lads drank their pints while I sat and mentally prepared myself for Millwall.

We were discussing how to get to the ground without the Old Bill latching onto us when I heard a car pull up outside. It was Millwall. I poked my head through the door to see what they wanted and this big, hard-looking geezer with a boxer's nose shouted over to me, asking me what I wanted to do.

'It's up to you. We're heading down the Old Kent Road later on. Feel free to come and see us.'

The Old Kent Road is the road that divides Bermondsey from the neighbouring districts of Camberwell, Peckham and Walworth. It's also where Millwall's main boozer, the Thomas a Becket, is.

'We'll be there,' the big fella sneered. 'Bring your firm, if you've got one.'

If we've got one? The cheeky bastard!

'Right. Drink up. We're off,' I told the rest of the lads.

This was usually the point where they would piss about for half an hour before finally getting their act together. This time, however, it was different. They gulped down their drinks and immediately headed towards the door. It was a sign we had come to do some real damage.

There are two ways of getting to The Den. You can either get the train to New Cross Gate, which is right next to the ground, or you can get off at New Cross station, half a mile further up the road. We decided it would throw the coppers off our scent if we got off at New Cross station. It's also only a five-minute walk from the Old Kent Road and it would give us a chance to bump into Millwall. The minute we got off, we were smack bang in the middle of their manor and as we got further into enemy territory, the houses started to look more and more run down and the locals began to resemble typical East End villains.

'Fuck me,' I whispered to Frankie. 'This is a fucking dodgy place.'

Bermondsey is the kind of area that proper blaggers come from, real ones, not the type that like to do a few post offices over every now and again. It's full of old railway arches, gloomy ginnels and side streets. The whole place looks like it was designed with hooligans in mind.

'Where are you lot from?' a grizzled old woman croaked as we pressed on towards the ground.

'Manchester,' I told her.

'Ha, ha, ha,' she cackled, 'Millwall are going to fucking murder you.'

I could feel the hairs on the back of my neck pricking with tension.

'You daft bastards. You're going to get eaten alive,' a woman pushing a buggy chimed in from across the street.

The whole of Bermondsey lived for football violence. Back in Manchester, it was a minority interest. In this neck of the woods it was clearly something that the entire population took great pride in.

Further down the road, a policeman clocked us and came across for a chat.

'Who are you lot then?' he asked.

'We're fackin' Millwall,' I told him, putting on my best Cockney accent. He looked confused. The fact that we'd got off at New Cross rather than New Cross Gate had clearly thrown him and part of him seemed to actually believe that we were locals. He still had an inkling that we were City fans but he couldn't work out why we were so far from the ground.

'Well, see that you don't cause any trouble.'

My Cockney accent must have been authentic. I'd managed to convince a Londoner that I was from the same place as him. One of Millwall's swag workers[18] overheard our conversation and advised us not to let their firm hear us claiming to be them.

'Just be careful. You'll get fucking killed down there,' he warned.

Ignoring him, we ploughed on round the corner straight into a load of their lads. They looked pissed off.

'You're not fackin' Millwall, you mug,' a big, scary-looking cunt bellowed in my face, obviously having heard our little pretence.

'No. We're the Young Guvnors,' I replied.

Within seconds, a good two hundred and fifty Millwall had formed a circle round us, making it impossible for us to retreat. It was jam-packed with them but it's weird because whenever you're in that situation there's always a foot-wide gap between you and them, an invisible barrier if you like.

'Let's have it then, you Northern slags,' one of their lads bellowed.

When you know that conflict is inevitable, you stop being afraid and you focus on the task at hand. I was eating a pie so I flung it into the nearest Millwall lad's face and watched him stagger back in pain. The pie was piping hot and the thick, brown gravy stuck to his skin and scalded him.

'If we've got a firm?' I yelled. 'This is our fucking firm.' With that, we surged forwards, lashing out at the cunts for all we were worth.

After a couple of minutes of fighting, we managed to get our hands on a portable metal fence and we launched it at Millwall. I didn't know it at the time but we'd been infiltrated by an undercover copper and

---

[18] A swag worker is somebody that sells merchandise before or after a match or a gig.

he was filming the whole thing. The footage of us hurling the fence would later be shown in court as part of the Operation Omega trial. It was the first time they'd used undercover policemen to bring down football-related gangs. Although we didn't know it then, that afternoon in south-east London was the beginning of the end for our firm.

Many of Millwall's lads were in their mid forties, a lot older than we were, and they looked like proper criminals. However their intimidating appearance wasn't going to prevent us from standing our ground and as soon as it was time for the match to start, we jumped the turnstiles and the fighting continued inside the stadium. Eventually, the police turned up and restored order.

Another group of City lads arrived shortly after the game had kicked off. Their coach had been smashed to fuck and had to be taken out of service. We were glad that they'd turned up though, as it helped even the numbers. We'd done all right considering that there were forty of us and a couple of hundred of them but now that we had a few more lads with us, we could show them what we were made of.

City won the game 1–0 but, to be honest, I can't remember much about the game itself, which is a recurring theme. Being a football fan is like being a music fan. When you're young and you're into a band, you want to know everything about them and you have their posters plastered all over your walls, whereas when you get older, you're still into the music but you appreciate it in a different way. You don't need to know the details of every last gig. You've gone beyond the stage where you need to prove your dedication.

After the game, Millwall's swag worker pulled us to one side and told us that their firm, the Bushwhackers, would be waiting for us at London Bridge station.

'Don't try and break the escort. Wait until the Old Bill have trailed off and then you can do whatever you want,' he told us.

We thanked him for the advice and set off down the Old Kent Road. Sure enough, the further away from the ground we got, the smaller the escort became and, by the time we got to the station, we were on our own. We were expecting a horde of Millwall to descend on us the second we opened the station doors but they were kind enough to give us a couple of minutes to find out where our train was leaving from.

We were pacing around the platform, wondering where they'd got to, when we heard a booming Cockney voice from across the tracks.

'You soppy Northern cunts. We're going to fackin' hammer you.'

Within a split second, the station had transformed itself into a battle-field and a hefty mob of Millwall was bowling its way across the bridge. We set off up the stairs to meet them and ended up clashing with them halfway down.

'Come on then you Cockney bastards,' I yelled, as I booted one of their lads back up the steps.

When you're faced with a snarling pack of rival lads, the rush is all-encompassing. It's similar to dropping ecstasy. There is a sudden surge of adrenaline, filling you to the brim with nervous energy. I was in my element, pummelling my fists into anybody who got in my way. It was the perfect end to the perfect day and as the transport cops came across to separate us, I remember thinking it would be great if every away game was like that.

Millwall had lived up to our expectations and then some. They were game as fuck but I'd say that we came out on top. It was a result and we were proper buzzing. We'd travelled to a place that was renowned for the high calibre of its hooligans and walked away with our heads held high.

By the time we finally managed to board our train, all we wanted to do was sleep. We were exhausted after everything we'd been through. There comes a point when you run out of adrenaline and your body crashes out.

Millwall are definitely in the top three London firms. I'd only put West Ham and Arsenal above them. They came out in force for us and did themselves proud. For a club of their size, they can pull hefty numbers. It was one of those games where even the most anti-hooligan of City fans was pleased to see us there. We made them feel safe and, without us there, they would have got done over. But did we get any thanks for keeping them safe?

You can guess the answer to that one.

12

HEADHUNTERS

London's a funny old place. It's easy to understand why there are so many hooligans in Millwall's manor but what about the richer areas where the bankers and the stockbrokers live? There are parts of the city where it costs £1 million to buy a one-bedroom apartment, which leads me to wonder where recreational violence fits in with the type of people who go to gastro pubs and shop at Harrods. Kensington and Chelsea is one of the capital's richest boroughs. It is also home to the Chelsea Headhunters, formerly one of the most feared firms in Britain. They've been all over the media ever since that prick Donal Macintyre wormed his way in with them (leading to the conviction of top Chelsea lad Jason Marriner) but despite the recent hype surrounding them, they are a shadow of their former selves. Nowadays they don't make the top five.

Back in the Eighties, Chelsea were a naughty firm and had a reputation for carrying a fearsome arsenal of weapons. It was usually chains, knives and knuckledusters but they would use whatever they decided to take along with them on the day. They had a real swagger, an intimidating self-confidence. There was something about the way they walked. It said, 'We're Chelsea and we're the fackin' Guvnors.' Obviously we were the fackin' Guvnors but when they strode around like that it was enough to give us a few doubts.

Chelsea travelled in ridiculous numbers to away matches. I remember when they came to Maine Road in May 1984. They were turning up throughout the afternoon, from about twelve o'clock. Every London train had Headhunters on it and we got cornered on the approach to

Piccadilly. Eight of us were standing there, minding our own business, when a load of Chelsea came marching out of the station. One of them turned around and smacked me in the mouth, taking me completely by surprise.

'You fackin' mugs,' he yelled, as his fist connected.

There was only a handful of us and we were just standing there. We weren't giving it the big 'un or anything. I hadn't expected them to kick off like that and I immediately bounced away from the wall so that I had room to get away. There were fucking hundreds of them, all of them big, hard-looking cunts.

'Look at the size of you, you daft twat,' I shouted, as I made my way down the road and out of harm's way. If I'd stuck around I would have ended up in hospital. What is it Johnny Cash sings about knowing when to fold 'em?

They hung around the city centre until the game was about to start and then made a beeline for our end. They didn't go into the Platt Lane stand; they would have got fucking murdered. But they took the main stand facing the Kippax, which was bad enough. They had some scary-looking blokes with them, all skinheads with Doc Martins and Fred Perry T-shirts. We didn't stand a chance. There were hundreds of the cunts.

When Chelsea scored their first goal, the scorer must have realised what was about to happen because he immediately signalled for their fans to stay where they were. Unfortunately for him, they ignored his plea and piled onto the pitch to celebrate. If you watch the match on YouTube, you can hear the commentator saying, 'Sadly, a handful of fans didn't take notice of him. Immediately after scoring the goal, he told the supporters to go off. What a lovely moment for him, because he showed what an intelligent footballer he is and what an intelligent man as well.' As if the fact that he'd ordered them to stay put had any bearing upon his intelligence!

When they scored their second, groups of Chelsea ran out onto the pitch from both directions. They must have been fucking pleased with themselves. They'd won the game and taken our seats. What more could they want? As it turns out, they wanted to kick the shit out of us as well. As soon as the match finished, it went off everywhere, and I mean everywhere. They had the biggest mob I've ever seen and we weren't prepared. They overran the whole city; they even turned up at our pub, the Cyprus.[19] I've got to hand it to them; they were unstoppable. The only result we got that day was smashing up their coaches, but, that apart, they annihilated us.

The second time we came across Chelsea's mob was during a match against Wimbledon on 25 August 1984, shortly after they'd managed to work their way up to the second division. Wimbledon had a proper non-league ground and it was easy for us to get into their end. We weren't expecting anything to kick off. We hoped that we'd end up rowing with somebody but we weren't holding out for anything special. So you can imagine our delight when it got to half time and a big group of City fans started looking behind them and singing, 'You're going to get your fucking heads kicked in.'

There was obviously another firm waiting for us outside the ground.

'Will all the away fans please look at the pitch?' the voice on the tannoy boomed. 'There's nothing happening over there.'

Yeah, right. Chelsea had played Arsenal earlier in the day and the Headhunters were out in force, looking for us. They were two hundred and fifty-strong and it was a shame because the Old Bill turned up before we had a chance to get stuck into them. Still, the gauntlet had been thrown and we weren't about to sit back and let them take the piss. It was time to head off into Wimbledon and find them.

We had a look about for Chelsea but they were nowhere to be seen so we decided to head to Victoria to get the train home. We were confused, wondering why they had wound us up and then got off. Little did we know they drank in a pub called the Shakespeare, in Victoria, and that they were planning on ambushing us as soon as we got there.

We were heading into the territory of London's most notorious hooligans, unaware that we were about to get the kicking of our lives.

---

[19] The Cyprus Tavern was opened in 1967 by Greek-Cypriot immigrant Takros Kitromilides. Although it started out as one of the city's first student-friendly pubs, it eventually became a focal point for different sets of hooligans. It was a moody place to go. They had an unofficial dress code – you weren't allowed in if you had an open wound, which was an indication of what the atmosphere was like!

Only one lad realised the danger we were in. He was pacing up and down the train, saying, 'We're all dead. We're all dead. We're going to get fucking hammered. We're going to get ambushed and kicked to fuck.' I thought, 'All right, calm down. There's no need to panic.' If I'd known what lay in store I would have been joining in. Instead I airily dismissed his concerns. To me it was much ado about nothing.

Sometimes our rivals would be waiting for us at the platform so that they could weigh us in the minute we came off the train but the Cockneys chose to leave it until we were going through the ticket barriers at Victoria before they made their move. We were just beginning to let our guard down when we heard a chant of 'Ooh, ooh, ooh,' echoing around the station. It was their way of letting us know that they meant business. Every firm has its own way of intimidating the opposition. If you can spook the other mob you are much more likely to run them.

Chelsea came from everywhere. We were badly outnumbered and as soon as we saw how many lads they had, we were off. We had no choice. I had an expensive jumper on and was I worried that they were going to steal it. The Londoners had a habit of taking the clothes off your back. They would kick the fuck out of you and then, adding insult to injury, walk off wearing your jacket. They were similar to the Scousers in that respect.

I managed to hide out in WH Smith until it was safe to make my retreat. I can remember looking through the window and seeing all these proper hard-looking geezers running around in big baggy jeans and long leather coats. They were ridiculously stylish. They had long hair with a curly bit at the front and they were wearing Adidas New York trainers, the in thing at the time. The Cockneys were always the height of fashion. The Scousers may have created the casual look but the Londoners were the trendsetters before that look caught on.

Fearsome as they were, Chelsea went to fuck after they started getting raided by the coppers. There were only one or two people holding their firm together and once their main faces were off the scene, they didn't know what to do with themselves. In 1987, Terence Last ended up getting ten years for organising a six-year campaign of football violence. He was one of their top lads and during his trial the

Headhunters were described as 'Some of the nastiest, most ruthless men for whom violence appeared a way of life.' That may have been the case in the Seventies and Eighties but they aren't like that today. They're a pale imitation of what they used to be. It's a shame because they were a force to be reckoned with.

Still, every dog has its day.

13

BATTLE AT THE WHALLEY

One of our most memorable clashes with the Munichs was when they trashed our pub in January 1987. The main reason it's memorable is because they never shut up about it. I also think it is a perfect illustration of how they nearly always outnumbered us, often by about ten to one. To cut a long story short, they brought a couple of thousand and only a handful of our lot stood against them.

One of their top lads, Jason Clarke, has agreed to give his version of the day's events on condition that I leave his account exactly as he wrote it. After that, I give *my* verdict on the epic battle of the Mancs, a battle that has spawned many myths and has become the stuff of legend. Here's what Jason has to say about what went down at the Whalley:

You can't beat a good FA Cup run. In the Eighties we were fucking shite in the league and our only chance of glory seemed to lie in this competition. To get our sneaky, shithouse neighbours first off was a bonus. The FA Cup seemed to bring out more of the older faces and the firm were bigger for away games because we would get a larger allocation of tickets than normal.

City's firm were fucking sneaky cunts and I can honestly say from the time when I was active that, firm on firm, they have never done United. We had to hunt them down every derby day without fail. We made it easy for them by drinking in the Grey Parrot in Hulme, which is their manor, but they never came once. In Jan 1987 I left the house at eight and we made our way into town. We headed into the cafés around Piccadilly for our brekkie, where we discussed where we would plot up to see if they were making an early move. By ten o'clock there were around five hundred United so we made a move to the edge of City's manor, as we heard that they were meeting at the Sherwood near Maine Road. We positioned ourselves between them and Old Trafford and occupied a few pubs: The Mancunian, Three Legs of Man and the Platford. By one we were numbering between seven and eight hundred and firmed-up big style. The mood was one of confidence and expectation. We had spotters out in cars and we knew where they were and where they were heading. All the while we got more and more hyped up.

About half past one the word went round that three hundred City had just landed in the Whalley hotel, which is a huge pub with the road splitting off either side of it. The Whalley was two streets away and here we were, all alone and with no Old Bill. Game on! This was it. All the times we had hunted them down over the years and here they were on a plate. They were oblivious to the destruction that was heading their way.

We were at the junction within five minutes and the few City that were on the street ran into the Whalley and shut the door. We swarmed around and began the worst destruction of a pub I have ever seen. The doors opened and City made a token effort to get out but United just steamed up the steps and smashed them back into the hotel, which was now being destroyed from within as well. The doors closed again and City started wazzing plates, bottles, glasses, tables and chairs through the windows at us. The hotel's outer wall was being pulled down at this point and bricks were being sent through the gaping holes in the side of the building. The sills in the bay windows, which were made of stone, were torn out too. A single patrol car came skidding to a halt and it was instantly smashed. The Old Bill reversed as quickly as he could and then we knew it was minutes until the TAG[20] units would be on the scene. City tried coming out again, led by a lad I know called CJ, who was waving a big blade about. He was swiftly set upon and smashed to fuck. City were finished. They were totally overwhelmed by the severity of the assault, although they had it coming, to be honest.

---

[20] Tactical Aid Group, a special patrol group trained in crowd control. They turned up in dark-blue minibuses with mesh over the windows and if you ask me they were a bunch of fucking thugs, the lot of them.

Right on cue the TAG vans turned up and we were off, chased by pure dibble who to seemed to follow us for what seemed like forever. I was on the verge of stopping as sprinting for a mile is just not my thing. I rounded a corner and dived into a butcher's in desperation. It had a healthy queue of panting customers, all of whom had the same idea as me. We made our way to Old Trafford and waited for City to turn up and what a sorry bunch they looked when they got there. Three hundred was down to a hundred. They were covered in claret and still had to negotiate Warwick Road, which was heaving as it was getting near to kick off. I forgot to mention that we had one hundred and fifty tickets bang in the middle of City's allocation of twelve thousand, which promised to be eventful. We met at the Dog and Partridge and our plan was to enter K stand as one, as we expected to have to fight our way in. In we went and guess what? No City! Not a single one of them was there so we got in and took our seats.

We were now in the heart of the City section and sang to let them know that we were there but even this had no effect. So, at half time, we all went downstairs where a few digs were given out but no major ruck. The second half would prove more exciting as Norman Whiteside would score the goal that would finally wake up the City fans. We went berserk when we scored, which set off a shower of bottles and missiles in our direction and a small smoke bomb, which hit me on the shoulder. We were in such a frenzy that it didn't matter. It was fucking brilliant and we loved it. We were taking the piss big time and City were fucking wounded.

We had shown them who ran this fucking town.

At full time City made a move by coming up into J stand, which was to our right over a four-foot dividing wall. We steamed straight across the wall and into them. Now running across seats and bodies has its pitfalls and my Adidas jeans came off between the folding seats. I had to try and pull them back on while scrambling over terrified straight members. City took off as quickly as they had appeared and snuck away to lick their wounds, as they had been on the end of our wrath all day. They were a broken firm and they went back to the Sherwood to muster up one last chance to salvage some sort of pride, as the day had been ours from the outset. We had made our way into town and took over the main pubs, including the Sawyers Arms on Deansgate, which was packed with lads. Then the revenge assault began.

By this stage, City's firm were back together and they had filled their pockets with bricks and bottles. They carried them the full two miles from the Sherwood and attacked the Sawyers at around eight. United blasted their way out no trouble and smashed the tables and chairs into any City who stood in their way. Items of furniture were later reported to be found as far away as Albert Square.

It was the final insult for City. They were chased out of town like dogs. We had shown that it was impossible for them to live with us, as has always been the case. We had caught them and given them a real going over, from which they never really recovered. This episode began five years of tit-for-tat attacks. They knew that they couldn't handle us mob to mob as they had been crushed decisively and comprehensively that day.

A footnote

The Whalley was so badly damaged that it was closed for three months. Although we had countless battles with City, this was the norm throughout the 80s and early 90s. They became so paranoid about being cornered that they used to meet on derby day. . . in Failsworth, Oldham!

What Jason has neglected to mention is that fifteen of us stood our ground outside the Whalley and refused to go inside the pub. We were shouting 'Get out here and fight, now,' but nobody was moving. My version of events is a little different. And it goes like this.

First of all, we have to be sneaky cunts because United's firm is almost always so much bigger than ours. Our sneakiness is one of our greatest strengths and I make no apologies for it. Now that I've got that off my chest, I can begin my story.

Derby days were my favourites, as they gave us a chance to have a pop at our sworn enemies, the glory hunters. It was a day when you would be hard pushed to hear a northern accent on the streets of Manchester, as there were swarms of United everywhere, like a plague of big red locusts. If you believe Jason's account of what went on, you will no doubt think that we spend all of our time hiding from their firm but, in reality, we were just as game as they were, if not more so given the disparity in numbers. In his book Tony O'Neill claims that we were scared of Man U's firm and that we never arranged any fights with them. If that is true then why were a handful of us willing to take on an army? Answer me that.

On the day of the Whalley incident, one hundred and fifty of us met up in Moss Side and we made our way over to the pub to get a couple of drinks in before the game. It was a convenient place to stop off, what with it being halfway between our manor and their ground. Unlike our rivals, we were all from Manchester, apart from the two Cockney blues and a lad from Clitheroe, who, rather unoriginally, we had nicknamed Clitheroe. We knew that United were going to turn up and we were stood outside the pub wondering where the fuck they had got to when a car pulled up. A group of their lads leaned out of the window and threw a load of calling cards at us.

'Two minutes. We're on our way,' shouted the driver.

Sure enough, within the blink of an eye, we were completely surrounded by United. There were three hundred Cockney Reds, fifty Lincoln Reds, fifty from Coventry and the rest were from Manchester, which was surprising in itself. There are three separate roads leading up to the Whalley and there were rival hooligans blocking every exit.

'Stand your ground,' I yelled.

A handful of our gamest lads stood with me and refused to move but the rest of the firm fucked off back inside the pub and barricaded the doors shut.

'Get out here, now,' I insisted.

They were having none of it. Not only had they run away and made the Guvnors look like a bunch of fannies but they'd also locked us out. Frustrated at the lack of support, I started booting the door and shouting for them to open up but not one of them moved an inch.

United started pelting the pub with bricks and bottles and one of our lads threw a chair out at them in retaliation so I snapped a leg off and prepared myself for the oncoming horde of Scum. That was the difference between City and United. We were willing to go up against an opponent when we knew we didn't stand a chance. By contrast Jason and his boys would always rely upon superior numbers.

By this stage it was do or die. I could stand there and let them walk over me or I could go down fighting.

'Let's have you then,' I shouted and with that I brought my makeshift baton smashing down into the face of the nearest United lad. He didn't move an inch. He just stood there and took it. He was either one of the hardest people I'd ever seen or the blow had scrambled his brain. Either way, it shitted me up and I decided to turn my attention elsewhere. I swung around and piled straight into a big group of United who were coming towards me from behind. I was being bombarded by kicks and punches from every angle. I'd been potted in the side of the head, blood was gushing everywhere and things weren't looking too good.

I was just beginning to think that I was going to end up going home in an ambulance when the Old Bill arrived and slapped a pair of cuffs on me. I remember thinking, 'thank fuck for that'. I would have been badly hurt if they hadn't have turned up. I was taken to Stretford police station, charged with public disorder and released half an hour later.

'That was quick,' I said to the copper.

'Well,' he explained, 'It's a derby day, isn't it?'

He had a point. They couldn't afford to fuck around. The streets of Moss Side and Old Trafford were a war zone.

I would have been out of there a lot sooner if my face wasn't pouring with blood. As it was, they had to check my ear out because it was leaking claret all over the place. I was lucky to have escaped with a couple of cuts and bruises. I could easily have been killed.

Jason is right in saying that the majority of our firm refused to come out of the pub but he neglects to mention the brave lads who stood and fought. I'm not going to hold it against the lads who stayed inside the Whalley. They had their reasons. All I'm saying is that we didn't all hole ourselves up. You can't tar us all with the same brush because there were one or two of us who refused to hide.

So there you have it. Two accounts of the same event, although that's not to say one is more accurate than the other. Maybe Jason was too caught up in what was going on to notice the things that stuck in my mind. He seems to think we've never done United but I guess that depends on your definition of 'being done'. Do you class a victory due to superior numbers as doing someone or do you give more kudos to the firm that stands its ground, despite being vastly outnumbered? I know which option I'd pick but that's just me and everyone has their own indicators of success and failure.

The question that United need to ask is whether any of them would have stayed outside the pub if there were a thousand City fans laying siege. We had a chance to get off and we didn't. They'd already told us they were on their way and we knew what type of numbers they were coming with. We did well for ourselves, considering how many of us there were. I fought my corner when the odds were stacked against me and that's something nobody can take away from me.

When you're fighting an enemy that outnumber you by at least five to one, there's no point in rushing into them. Whenever United let their guard down, we were there to wipe the smiles off their faces. They may have trashed our pub but there have been times when we've done the same thing to them. I remember when we smashed up three of their boozers in a single evening. There was no music on in the Cyprus that night and there were lads grabbing the mic and yelling, 'City are back,' right up until last orders. They can rub the Whalley in our faces as much as they like but we've won our fair share of battles over the years.[21]

The fact that we stood against them meant that we'd won before we even started. Besides there are worse things than getting done at a derby. The only person who had ever truly cared about me was about to pass away and there was nothing I could do to stop it.

It was time to come face to face with my worst nightmare.

---

[21] The last game of the season in May 1989 when we were at Bradford and were promoted back to the first division springs to mind. United's lads know exactly what I'm on about.

14

TOO PRECIOUS TO REPLACE

I still remember the first time I realised something was wrong with my nana. It was a Friday night and I'd been staying over at her place to keep her company. I was lying on the couch trying to get some sleep when I heard her footsteps in the hallway. She let out a breathless cry for help, pleading with me to call an ambulance.

'Andrew,' she wheezed. 'I can't breathe. I'm in pain.'

A wave of panic washed over my body.

'Do you want me to go to the woman next door and wake her up?' I asked, attempting to ascertain just how sick she was.

'Yes. Go and get help.'

At that point I knew she was really poorly. She would never have agreed to wake the neighbours up unless she was in excruciating pain. I hurriedly flung my shoes on and flew out of the house.

'Open up,' I yelled, hammering my fists against the neighbour's door.

The minute the latch was off I sprinted into the house and grabbed the phone. There was no time for small talk. If I didn't act fast there was a real chance that my nana might die. I dialled 999 and started reeling off instructions.

'Send an ambulance straightaway. It's my nana. She's in a lot of pain. She's getting pains in her chest and she's having trouble breathing.'

The ambulance arrived fairly quickly and I accompanied my nana to the hospital, unwilling to leave her side. She'd had a heart attack and it was touch and go whether she was going to make it through the night. I was so afraid. I couldn't imagine what life would be like without her. I would have gone into the ward if they'd let me but I had to take a seat in the waiting room until they'd finished trying to save her.

After what had seemed like an eternity, a doctor came into the seating area and asked me how old I was.

'Eighteen,' I murmured, praying to god he wasn't going to tell me that my nana had died.

'Okay, you can go through and see her,' he told me.

Presumably the fact that I was allowed into the ward meant she was fit enough for me to see her. She had survived and I had saved her life. If I hadn't called the ambulance when I did then she probably wouldn't have made it.

When I finally arrived by my nana's side, I was close to tears. She had pipes coming out of her nose and mouth and she looked incredibly weak. I wanted to cry but I knew that I had to be strong. If I'd have started bawling my eyes out it would have upset her and that was the last thing I wanted to do. She held my hand in hers and squeezed it tightly, as if to assure me that she was going to be all right.

'Do you want me to go and get my dad?' I asked her.

She squeezed my hand again, a clear yes in my mind.

'Okay. Don't worry. I'll be right back.'

It was five in the morning and the buses hadn't started running. There was only one thing for it. I'd have to run all the way back to Gorton as fast as my legs could carry me. I was relieved that Nana had survived the night but at the same time panicking that she'd been left alone in a strange environment. A deep sense of unease was setting in. I was worried that I might still lose her.

The minute I got to Dad's house, I hammered on the door, desperate to get back to the ward as quickly as possible. After a couple of minutes of knocking, I saw a dark figure moving towards the window.

'What the fuck are you doing waking me up at this time?' Thea shouted, conjuring up a plethora of painful childhood memories. She was the last person I wanted to see.

'It's my nana. She's in hospital,' I told her.

Surely even a cold-hearted bitch like Thea could appreciate that the possibility of losing a relative was a pretty daunting prospect.

'You inconsiderate bastard,' she bellowed. 'Come back at a reasonable hour and stop making such a godawful racket.'

I didn't have time for Thea's shit.

'Listen you fucking bitch,' I yelled. 'Get my fucking dad down here NOW!'

Realising that I wasn't going away until the situation had been resolved, she reluctantly trundled off to wake Dad. She was a right evil cow and I'll never forget the way that she spoke to me that day. I hadn't expected words of comfort but she could at least have refrained from insulting me.

As soon as Dad arrived on the scene, I quickly explained the situation and we rushed to the hospital to see how my nana was doing. By the time we got there, she had suffered another massive heart attack but somehow made a full recovery.

'Is she going to be okay?' I asked the doctor.

'She's fine. We just need to keep her in for a few weeks to monitor progress.'

As we left the hospital, I felt that things had worked out for the best. Nana had pulled through and she was on the road to recovery. I didn't want to leave her but I knew she'd be in safe hands. Now it was time for me to leave her in peace until the doctors gave her the all clear.

I intended to visit her at the earliest opportunity, which was the following Monday. I rang the hospital a couple of hours in advance, to check if everything was okay. I wanted to speak to my nana directly, rather than relying upon the second-hand information provided by the doctors.

'Um, who are you and er. . . why do you want to speak to her?' stuttered the female voice on the other end of the phone.

'I'm her grandson. I want to hear her voice.'

Something wasn't right. I could sense it. Why was there so much humming and hawing?

'You need to come to the hospital,' she told me, 'and um. . . bring your dad as well.'

Alarm bells were ringing. There was obviously something the matter. Why else would they have told me to come to the ward before visiting time? Rather than immediately setting off for the hospital, I decided to go to my nana's house first to check if everything was all right there. The sooner I found out what was going on, the quicker my mind would be put at rest.

When I arrived at my nana's, there was a note pinned to the door saying, 'Andrew, don't go to the hospital.' It was in my dad's handwriting. A cold chill ran down my spine. I was now sure that something bad had happened. I made myself a sandwich and tried to calm down but it was difficult to think straight. If she had taken a turn for the worse the betting was she wouldn't be home any time soon. I was sick with worry.

My dad came to the door and broke the news that my nana had passed away. I remember a cold, dark wave washing over me, draining me of emotion. I understood what I'd been told but when I tried to think about the implications, my head went fuzzy, as if I didn't know what to make of it.

As the confusion turned into anger, I hurled my sandwich into the wall and stormed off into the living room. I thought I was going to go off on one but I didn't. I just slumped down into the settee with tears streaming down my face. I tried to speak but no sound came out. How do you express a loss that great? My heart had been wrenched out of my chest and thrown across the kitchen, along with the sandwich.

'Do you want a smoke?' Dad asked me.

I nodded. We sat there and smoked a pack of Silk Cut between us, unable to utter a single word. Nana had passed away minutes before I'd rung through to the hospital. No wonder the receptionist had been so strange. It must have been a difficult situation to deal with. How do you break the news to someone that the person they want to speak to is no longer alive? I glanced at my old man. For the first time I saw tears in his eyes. My dad's a hard man, not physically but emotionally. He chooses to handle things by holding them in.

'I've got to go,' he told me. 'Do you fancy a walk?'

'Why not?' I thought. Maybe a bit of fresh air would help to clear my head.

Everything that I walked past on the way to Dad's house reminded me of my nana. As we passed my old primary school, the memories came flooding back. She used to have fresh pies delivered from the cake shop every day and I'd run down the street at dinnertime, eager to eat my fill. I pictured Nana's smiling face, beaming down at me as I rushed to greet her. So much for clearing my head. Everything in Gorton had a little piece of her attached to it. It sounds daft but she was a mother to me as well as a nana. She's the only positive female role model I've ever had and I felt as if I'd lost a part of myself that day. She instilled a sense of right and wrong in me that is still there today. All the good in me comes from her.

Some things are far too precious to replace and my nana was one of those things. As we walked past the park, I thought back to when she used to push me on the swings. The song says that 'you don't know what you've got 'til it's gone' but I'd always known she was someone very special. All good things come to an end and Nana was no exception. I just wished that she could have lived a few years longer so that I would have had the chance to tell her how much I'd miss her. She was irreplaceable. Words can't begin to describe how much she meant to me.

As we approached Dad's house, all my fond memories faded away. There was nothing remotely positive about the place where I'd been neglected and abused for all those years at the hands of my evil bitch of a stepmother. I hoped that she wasn't in but, at the same time, I knew deep down that she'd be there and, sure enough, the minute the door opened, she was on my case.

'What's he doing here?' she asked Dad.

'His nan's just died. Can he come in for five minutes?'

My stepmam shot me a look of disgust.

'Okay five minutes,' she snapped. 'Make sure it's no longer than that. I've got things to do.'

I sat myself down on a stool in the kitchen and Dad went to make us a cup of tea.

'What are you doing?' Thea scowled. 'There's no milk. He can't have anything.'

There was a crate next to the door containing seventeen pints of the stuff. I couldn't believe how heartless she was. I wanted to cry but, at the same time, I didn't want to give her the satisfaction of knowing that she'd finally managed to get to me.

'You know what? It doesn't matter. I don't think I'm going to stay for the full five minutes.'

As I walked back down the same set of memory-laden streets, I had never felt more alone. It dawned on me that my nana had been the only person who had loved me no matter what. That kind of unconditional love is so rare. She was a wise woman. Normally, when somebody gave me advice, I spurned it. But when my nana told me something, I'd listen.

I carried on living at my nana's house for two weeks after she died, unable to accept the fact that she was gone. Sometimes I'd cry myself to sleep and dream that she was still alive. She'd be laughing and running around and it would feel as if everything was back to normal. Then, when the heating under the floorboards clicked on, I'd wake up, thinking I'd heard her getting up to go to the toilet. I was in a state of mental torment and everywhere I looked there were things that reminded me of her. Her half-eaten toastie, a shopping list she had written, a hairbrush with strands of her hair on it. It was too much to take.

Nana was the only person who had ever believed in me. Everybody else had always told me that I was thick or a bad influence or a born criminal. The rest of the world could go fuck itself as far as I was concerned though. My nana's opinion was the only one I ever cared about. If people thought I was a bad lad then they could hardly be surprised when I torched their car or when they saw me coming towards them with my hood up on a dark night, ready to slash them or beat the fuck out of them with a bat or a chain. People adapt to how society perceives them. Label me a monster and that's exactly what I'll be.

I had no money left for food and I'd eaten everything that my nana had left behind. I was starving, I was grieving and I was alone; life was shit. As the days passed, I got more and more desperate for cash. I'd been too depressed to go out grafting and I was literally penniless. Despite my reputation as someone who would steal anything that wasn't tied down, I hadn't even thought to search Nana's house for money. Even though she was dead, I still felt there was something inherently wrong about disturbing her belongings, although as my belly became emptier, it crossed my mind that she might have hidden something under the mattress.

Bingo! There was a bag of five-pence pieces. It was only a fiver's worth but it'd keep me going until I summoned up the motivation to find another source of income. Thinking that she might have stashed some more money somewhere, I lifted up the carpet and, lo and behold, there was a big stack of bank notes hidden underneath. It was as if she had wanted to provide me with one last gift to remember her by.

If Thea had been a proper mother to me then I wouldn't have needed to go rooting around my nana's house to get a meal. She'd made things ten times harder for me. There were no words of comfort offered towards me, only scowls and sly little putdowns. I felt lonely and isolated, as if nobody truly understood what I was going through. That spiteful cow knew exactly what I'd been made to endure and she couldn't have cared less. She was a fucking bitch and she could burnt in hell, for all I cared.

As it happened, I got my wish sooner than I had expected, as Thea developed a terminal form of cancer at the tender age of fifty-two. I can remember when my old man rang to tell me what had happened. I felt sad that he was about to lose the person that he loved but, at the same time, I was pleased that she was finally on her way out.

'You need to book her a hotel room,' I told him. 'Get her out of the hospital. You don't want her to die in there.'

She meant a lot to him. If he hadn't felt so strongly about her I would have danced round the room but as it was I didn't know how to feel. On the one hand I was excited that I was finally going to be rid of her but, on the other, the damage had already been done and nothing could reverse the pain she had inflicted on me. My dad was pulling out all the stops to make her last days on earth as pleasurable as possible, whereas when my nana died Thea had argued about whether or not he could make me a cup of tea. If it had been up to me, I would have left her to rot.

Sure enough, a couple of weeks down the line, my dad rang to say that Thea had passed away.

'Can I go to the funeral?' I asked, trying hard to disguise my relief.

'Her family don't want you to go. They know that you didn't get on with her and they don't think it would be right for you to be there.'

I wanted to see her getting lowered into the ground. Not in a sadistic way, I just needed to know that she was never coming back. When my nana had died, I'd seen her in the hospital with pipes coming out of her nose, but this time it just didn't seem real to me. A single phone call, that was all I had to go on. I needed to see Thea's lifeless body so that I could finally get her out of my head.

The fact that I didn't get to witness Thea being buried weighed heavily on my mind over the next few months. Ideally, I would have liked to have let her know exactly what I thought of her before she died. She'd only survived as long as she had because I'd allowed her to live. I could have banged her out at any moment.

I never had the chance to ask her what she had against me and the closure I would have got from attending the funeral had been withheld. I was still worried that she would walk back into my life, proclaiming that she had been alive the whole time.

They say the death of a loved one can meddle with your sanity. Well let me tell you, the death of an enemy can be just as bad. I couldn't get to grips with the fact that the loudmouthed bitch who had abused me for years had left the earth so discreetly. That was when the nightmares started. I'd see her face leering at me whenever I closed my eyes. I'd wake up in a cold sweat, feeling that she was tormenting me from beyond the grave. While the dreams about my nana had comforted me, the idea that my stepmam might still be out there chilled me to the bone.

After a while, I started seeing Thea when I was awake as well as when I was asleep. I saw a bus driver who looked like her and I almost had a heart attack; I nearly did the fella in. This supernatural mumbo jumbo had to stop.

That night, I decided to issue a challenge to whatever was causing me so much grief.

'Okay. I'm going to run the bath and then I'm going to put my head under the water. If you're a ghost and you're haunting me then hold it under and kill me. If you don't do anything then I'll know you aren't real. This is what you want, isn't it? Do your fucking worst.'

I filled the bathtub with warm water, plunged my head beneath the surface and braced myself for a pair of skeletal hands to appear from out of thin air and try to do me in. Nothing happened. 'Come on. If you're going to do it then this is your chance.' Still nothing. When I finally came up for air, I knew that she had definitely gone because if she could have killed me she would have done. It was over. I was no longer 'that bastard'. I was Benny of Gorton and I was free.

I still have dreams about my stepmam every now and again,

although these days when she tries to intimidate me, I say, 'Look you silly cow. I spared your life. I could have broken every bone in your body but I didn't. You've got me to thank that you survived as long as you did.'

And it's true. The emotions I experienced when I found out that she had died couldn't have been further removed from how I felt when I was told that my nana had passed away. You reap what you sow. Rest in peace Nana. I'd like to say the same to Thea but I doubt it's peaceful where she's gone.

The trials and tribulations of my early life fuelled my passion for hooliganism. When you're in the heat of battle, your troubles seem meaningless and the only thing that you care about is coming out on top. Football violence alleviated the pain of losing my nana and it rendered meaningless the hurtful things that Thea had said to me. It was Novocain for the soul.

Even the times when we got battered provided me with a release from the grim realities of everyday life and one team in particular gave us a run for our money whenever they crossed our path. Every firm has a team that they secretly dread going up against and in our case it was a mob that were very similar to the Guvnors. They were a multiracial unit from a tough city, they travelled in numbers, they played in blue and they were game as fuck. I'm talking about the firm that took their name from a tribe of African warriors.

The Birmingham City Zulus, one of the best mobs I've had the misfortune to come across.

15

THE ZULUS

The Zulus was a fresh-faced young firm that was always eager to prove itself. Whereas a lot of mobs could talk the talk but weren't much good at backing up their threats, we had our work cut out whenever we played Birmingham. 'Zulu, Zulu, Zulu'. It was an intimidating thing to hear echoing round a railway station and the minute you came within earshot of the chant, you were in trouble. I remember when City played Newcastle and one of the Geordie lads told me that there were only a handful of firms he rated and that one of them was Birmingham. As far as I'm concerned being complimented on your fighting by a Geordie is the ultimate accolade. The Zulus are one of the best mobs that I've come up against and they've done us on a number of occasions.

The first time the Brummies got one over on us was on 10 November 1984 when they came to Maine Road and leathered us on our home turf. It was a shock to the system. We'd been under the impression we'd always get the upper hand against anyone that ventured into our territory. I remember it like it was yesterday. A defeat like that never goes away. It taught us a lesson to be doubly prepared when the Zulus came to town.

It started out like any other match day. We met at the Sunspot arcade, just at the bottom of the approach to Piccadilly station, and hung out there until they got in. The arcade was the perfect spot to while away the time before an opponent touched down. It gave us the chance to make a bob or two before it kicked off and we'd be fiddling the machines right, left and centre, trying to earn enough to pay for transport to the next away game.

The Zulus arrived at eleven and they were a sight to behold. They were dressed from head to toe in Burberry and they were nearly all black. A fair few of them had Burberry golfing umbrellas and they looked fucking impressive. We were straight into them, doing our best to show them that we didn't give a fuck how well turned out they were. They were in our city and they were going to go home bleeding all over their nice new designer clothes. We went toe to toe but they quickly got the upper hand and, before long, a couple of our lads had made a beeline for the Arndale centre. We'd only been having it with them for a matter of minutes and they'd already got us on our toes.

As I struggled to drag myself through the doors of the Arndale, I felt a volley of blows raining down upon me from every angle. Them umbrellas don't half hurt! You wouldn't have thought a golf umbrella could do that much damage but it's like being hit with a solid-steel baton. By the time I'd made my way inside, I was bruised from head to toe. The Zulus were hot on my tail and they soon caught up with me. The entrance to the Arndale has two adjacent escalators, one going up and one going down and some of the lads had managed to make their way to the top level before changing their minds and deciding that they wanted to come back down. We couldn't make up our minds whether to stay or whether to make a run for it. On the one hand we wanted to keep our pride intact but, on the other, we knew deep down that we were going to get weighed in if we hung about.

Most of the lads managed to leg it up the escalators but a couple of us got gripped by the Brummies and we ended up getting kicked to fuck. It was proper embarrassing. They were on our manor and we should have been all over them. We'd failed in our duty to protect our home turf, although there was still time to turn things around.

'We can't be having this,' I ranted. 'We're Man City. Let's get ourselves to Maine Road and do the cunts.'

We were bruised and we were bloody but we weren't beaten yet. The real battle was still to come and we were determined to come out on top.

Unwilling to admit defeat, we jumped aboard the number 76 bus and set off for round two. Rather than distributing ourselves evenly throughout the vehicle, we positioned ourselves at the front of the lower deck, ready to jump out and ambush them if the opportunity arose. As we approached the stadium, we could see a big mob of Zulus stood outside the ticket office, taking pictures of one other. They were no doubt intending to use the photos as evidence that they'd been able to travel through our territory without being challenged. We were straight into the bastards. We didn't care that they'd managed to photo themselves. It didn't come into the equation. We were just buzzing that another pop was on the cards.

There were a hundred City and around a hundred and fifty Zulus. They were out in force and I've got to give them credit for bringing so many boys with them. There were a couple of Old Bill on the scene but we ignored them. Unless they had cameras we wouldn't even acknowledge their existence. After all, what's a single copper going to do to two hundred and fifty hardened thugs? If they had dogs it was a different story because nobody wants to get on the wrong side of a vicious Alsatian. However, they were run-of-the-mill cops and powerless to stop us.

We managed to back the Brummies off towards the Kippax and for the first couple of minutes it looked like we were going to even the score. Just as I was beginning to think that we were on the verge of retrieving the situation, I heard a slow, deep chant of 'Z-U-L-U' coming from the other end of the street. There was another mob of the fuckers sneaking up behind us. I turned around to see how many of them there were and I was immediately struck hard in the face with an umbrella. My nose erupted into a waterfall of claret, staining my clothes a dark shade of crimson. We were surrounded, outnumbered, outwitted and outdone. There was nowhere to run to. We were fighting for survival.

It's frightening when you're scrapping with a big mob and all of a sudden another group comes up behind you. It makes you wonder if a third, or even a fourth, wave of the cunts is round the corner, ready to weigh you in. By now the fight was in full flow. Lads were getting punched, kicked, bricked and twatted with umbrellas. They had us trapped like mice in a cage. We were getting a fucking pasting.

Eventually the dibble turned up mob-handed and escorted the Zulus to their end. I've got to hand it to the Brummies. They had leathered us twice before the game had even started. Some of the lads were trying to make excuses but if you don't admit your failings then you'll never improve as a firm. There are certain firms that will bombard you with excuses when you get the better of them. The Red Army is a prime example. It's always 'We were outnumbered' or 'It wasn't our main mob' or 'We weren't at home, wait till we get you at Old Trafford.' But people who say that aren't fooling anyone. It's better to say 'Yeah, all right, we got twatted but we've learned from the experience and we'll do better next time.'

During the game, we were half expecting the Zulus to come into our seats. If we'd been in their position, we would have gone into their end and battered them, just to emphasise our dominance. Luckily for us, we didn't see them again until the ninety minutes were up. They were obviously more concerned with watching the match, which, unfortunately for them, City won 1–0. As soon as the final whistle had blown and we were outside, they were straight back into us, kicking and punching us as we made our way along Lloyd Street and back towards town.

This time, the Old Bill knew what to expect, and within minutes, they had dragooned the Brummies into an escort, which meant that all they could do was shout and swear at us from behind a wall of dibble. When firms give you abuse from inside an escort they're usually glad you can't get at them. The Zulus were a different kettle of fish. You could see the hunger in their eyes and I knew without a shadow of a doubt that they were genuinely baying for our blood.

The police were determined to prevent the two firms from clashing again and they stayed with the Brummies all the way to Piccadilly, where they put them on their train. It would have been a foolproof solution but the Zulus were more concerned about fighting with us than about getting home. As soon as the coppers had fucked off, they got off the train and headed along the footbridge towards the platform where we had congregated. It was our fourth row with them in less than six hours, making it one of the most eventful days we've ever had.

Rather than heading up the steps, we waited halfway down the platform so that we could run at them the second they reached the bottom. The moment their feet touched the floor, we made our move, trying our hardest to avoid their umbrellas as we rained a volley of blows down on them. There aren't too many firms that will pile straight back in after having the living fuck kicked out of them a couple of hours earlier. We put up a decent effort and while we may not have succeeded in turning the Brummies over we showed them that we were willing to defend our city.

Eventually, the Old Bill turned up for the umpteenth time and the action came to a halt. They waited with us until our train got in and we were sent on our way without having made any real impression on the visitors. There was only one thing for it. We would have to turn out in force the next time we played them. We couldn't have them thinking they could waltz into our city, batter us and leave as if nothing had happened. This time we'd be ready.

The next match was on 3 September 1985, on their home turf. It was a chance to redeem ourselves. We'd suffered a crushing defeat when they came to Maine Road and if we didn't get a result this time round it would be tantamount to admitting they were a better firm. A massive mob of us met at Piccadilly at around half past three, determined to regain our stolen pride. It was time to give the Zulus a taste of their own medicine.

The police were onto us the minute our train pulled up at the station in Birmingham and we were immediately herded into an escort. We knew the Old Bill would eventually leave us alone, provided we behaved, and we did our best to convince them we weren't going to cause trouble. By the time we got to the stadium, there were only a couple of coppers left on our case and we were basically free to do as we pleased.

Nothing was kicking off outside St Andrew's so we jumped the turnstiles and went into their seats. It was a sure-fire way of starting a row. It was always scary going into another mob's end because you never knew what would be waiting for you but then again the fear of the unknown made it so much more exciting. We were intrepid explorers, venturing into enemy territory and I was buzzing my tits off about what was on the other side of that stile.

Once we were inside, Donald Francis led the way and we walked into the seats as a united mob. We marched straight to the front of the terracing, turned around and shouted, 'Come on Birmingham. We're

Man City!' All eyes were on us and, for a couple of seconds, their firm looked aghast, with their mouths wide open, wondering what the fuck was going on. Meanwhile, the City scarfers in the away end started chanting 'City aggro, City aggro,' and the entire place descended into chaos. The police moved towards us and from the other direction the Zulus charged down the steps, incensed at our audacity.

It was a good few minutes before there were enough dibble on the scene to separate the warring sets of fans and, by that stage, the violence had spilled onto the pitch. As the Old Bill were leading us back round to the away end, the Brummies were looking on in complete disbelief, as if they couldn't get their heads around it. I was grinning from ear to ear. We'd got in for free, we'd gone in their end and we'd got a result. What more could we have asked for? It's always so satisfying to get one over on a mob that has given you a beating in the past. I was fucking made up and the rest of the firm felt the same way.

Birmingham is by far the best of the Midlands firms. Forest is the only other mob that comes close. I don't rate Villa. We've been in their seats and they didn't even try to stop us, something that their city neighbours, the Zulus, would never have put up with.

It's always gratifying to come up against a worthy opponent and the Zulus are certainly in that category.

16

A DAY AT THE SEASIDE

I remember more about our antics on the terraces than I do about the football. When you follow a side that are as shit as City were, you have to look for excitement elsewhere. If I'd concentrated on our performances on the pitch, I would have topped myself. We managed to pluck defeat from the jaws of victory at every opportunity.

One of the few matches I was genuinely excited about was away to Blackpool in the third round of the FA Cup on 7 January 1984. Frankie was on the phone the second the balls were pulled out of the bag, asking if I'd seen who we'd drawn.

'Yeah. It'll be a walkover,' I told him.

Blackpool were in the fourth division, we were in the old second division. We should have been able to beat them no trouble. But, City being City, things never went according to plan.

Although I didn't expect for a single minute that we'd lose to Blackpool, their mob was a different kettle of fish. They had a reputation for being a tidy little firm and I'd heard about the tear ups that they'd been having with Wigan.

We set off to Blackpool double early so that we'd arrive in town before the Five-O. We jibbed the train by buying half tickets and spent the entire journey discussing how we were going to get to the ground without the Old Bill getting onto us. The minute we reached the station, I was peering out of the windows to see if there were any officers on the platform.

'It's all clear. Not a copper in sight,' I announced.

It was only half nine and we had time to kill. Frankie and Little

Spinner headed over to the arcades to make a raise. Nobles had a deal on where you could get a breakfast and a cuppa for a pound so we grabbed something to eat while we were there. I got myself a big plate of egg, beans and sausage and a cup of tea. The cut-price food was the owners' way of enticing people in so that they'd gamble their hard-earned money away. But that only works when your clientele aren't fiddling the machines. We must have cost them a small fortune by the time we'd had our fill.

A lad called Ersk[22] was seeing a girl from Blackpool and he had got to know a couple of their firm. We dispatched him to tell them where we would be plotted up and then hung around at the station, waiting for them to show their faces. Sure enough, at half ten, we saw a hundred and fifty Blackpool striding towards us. There were only seventy Guvnors, most on the young side.

This would be a day to remember.

'Benny,' shouted one of Blackpool's mob.

How the fuck did he know my name? They must have had one of United's lot with them. That's the only explanation I can think of. Some firms like to yell your name out to attract your attention. It's fucking dodgy though as it lets the Old Bill know who you are.

Me and Little Spinner walked straight into the middle of Blackpool's firm without a pause for thought. They could carry on shouting 'Benny' until they were blue in the face. It was no skin off my nose.

---

[22] You may have noticed that I haven't included Ersk in the list of Young Guvnors at the front of this book. That's because he is a fucking coward and he was never really one of us. He could talk the talk but when it kicked off, he was one of the first lads to run. People thought that he could handle himself because he was a big lad but he's a fucking bed wetter. He later went on to grass me up and caused me no end of bother. I'd missed a court appearance and the sly bastard went and rang the coppers up and told them where I was. He'd just had my mate off on five hundred quid and he was worried that I was going to bring it on top for him so he deliberately leaked my whereabouts to the Five-O. The cheeky fucker came and sat next to me on the bus a couple of years later and tried to pretend nothing had happened. I waited until he'd got to his stop and then I chased the grassing bastard all over Manchester. He's always been a fucking queer and, as far as I'm concerned, he was never one of the lads, even when he used to knock about with us.

'Come on then,' I bellowed. 'Let's have you.'

I didn't need to ask them twice. They were well up for it. Me and Spinner managed to back them off but we were quickly surrounded and pummelled from every direction. It was weird because they'd formed a semi-circle around us but, at the same time, the rest of our lads were on the other side of them. Rather than weighing in straightaway, they had chosen to leave it until our opponents were busy fighting with us to give them the element of surprise when they finally made their move.

Blackpool were no mugs. They stood their ground once the main body of our firm hit them and they did their best to fend us off. But it wasn't long before we had them on their toes. Credit where it's due, they were straight back in as soon as they regained their composure. Every time we got stuck in they would fall back, regroup and come at us again. This continued all the way to Bloomfield Road, where they finally fucked off and left us in peace.

It was time to rob ourselves some tickets.

Luckily for us one of the lads was able to snatch a parcel full of briefs[23] from the office, leaving us time for one last pop at our rivals before the game kicked off. While the rest of the mob were sorting through the tickets, me, Larry, E.T., Rodney and Little Spinner nipped off to find out where their firm had got to. They weren't hard to find. In fact they were mobbed up to fuck and they now had a good two hundred-odd lads in tow.

'Come on then you dickheads,' Larry shouted. We always liked to wind our opponents up before we had it. It got them nice and angry, ensuring that they fought their hardest.

We started off by throwing rocks, which kept them at bay for a while and then, when we'd run out of missiles, we made our way back to the ground, where the rest of our lads were waiting. Soon enough, the two full mobs were at it, refusing to back down. It wasn't like the last time. Both sides refused to budge and the violence carried on for several minutes. Eventually, the Old Bill turned up with dogs and horses, determined to put a stop to the disorder. They managed to split us up, which was a shame because it's not very often that two

---

[23] 'Briefs' is our slang for tickets. I don't mean a parcel of undies.

firms will stand without either of them losing its bottle. Blackpool were worthy opponents.

Their team didn't do too badly either.

As I walked into City's end, I was confident we would win. We weren't the best team in the world but we were up against a side that was even shitter than us. Besides, it was about time we won something.

Imagine my horror when Blackpool scored an early goal. I was fucking gutted. Typical City. And then the Tangerines snatched a second. The final nail in the coffin. We were fucked.

The home support wasn't making things any easier. They gesticulated at us and launched volleys of coins into our end. Two could play that game.

'Right, smash the roof in and we'll chuck the pieces that come off at them,' I told the rest of the Guvnors.

Within minutes, we'd broken off hefty chunks of roof asbestos and we were picking the debris up, ready to pelt them. What did they expect? They were taking the piss. Cheeky bastards.

After a brief exchange of projectiles, a grossly overweight copper made his way into no man's land and started bellowing orders. It was an open invitation for me to bombard him with asbestos too. PC Fat Cunt was one of those dibble who like to think they're a cut above. I took great pleasure in demonstrating to him that he was the same as everyone else. Both sets of fans were getting pelted with debris so it was only fair that he should have some as well. Fat Cunt turned red as a beetroot and shot me a look of disgust. I scowled back and levelled another chunk of roofing at the silly bastard's head. He could do fuck all about it and I kept on hurling the asbestos at him until he threw in the towel and hotfooted out of range.

While this was going on, City finally pulled their finger out and scored. It was of little consequence. We were obviously going to lose and it didn't matter if we lost by one goal or a million goals. The only way that we could make up for our poor performance on the pitch was by getting a result against Blackpool's mob.

The local police force didn't have a clue how to handle us and in the end they had to bring in the Merseyside Old Bill. The Scouse police were better equipped to deal with us and they eventually managed to put a lid on things. It didn't last long because, the minute we got outside, all hell broke loose again. Windows were put through, shops were looted and every hotel in the vicinity was smashed to fuck. One of the Guvnors even ended up doing a jewellery store over, which brought even more coppers out. We were furious at losing the game but we were made up to have caused such a major disturbance. For that reason it was a game to remember.

As far as Blackpool's firm was concerned, we didn't see them after the game, although that was partly because we had to get out of town quickly after causing so much damage. Never mind, we reasoned, we had managed to ransack their arcades, trash their hotels, overturn a car and do a fair few smash and grabs. All things considered it had been a blast.

A couple of months down the line, Eric Towner of the *Manchester Evening News* wrote a piece entitled 'Soccer's Secret Squads of Scum', partially inspired by the trouble that we'd caused in Blackpool. He described the fight we'd had with their firm and he spoke in great detail about how he had supposedly risked his life by meeting us at a 'secret address' in a rundown area of Manchester. Had he fuck. He'd met a couple of the lads at Spinner's flat in Whalley Range, which was hardly some kind of secret Guvnors hideout. At the end of the article, the paper includes a quote from the Lancashire police, which confirms that, 'It was exactly as the young thug described it.' In other words, the Guvnors *had* gone to Blackpool and wrecked the place. If I give an account of what's gone on you can rest assured it's accurate. I've got nothing to prove and I've got no reason to tell lies to big myself up. I've been in my fair share of battles over the years and I have the scars to prove it.

We were naïve in a way because we didn't ask for a penny for the information we gave to the *Evening News*. It was a centre-page spread as well so it would have been worth a few bob. We were milked for our stories and then the paper told the world that we were 'scum', without so much as a measly couple of quid to compensate us. What a fucking joke.

When you following a team that always lets you down, you can either stand around moping or you can make up for it in other ways. City the team may have lost to Blackpool, but City the firm were one of the gamest sets of lads that you were ever likely to come across. The Guvnors got a result that day. We fucking hammered them. We trashed their town and we stamped our authority on them good and proper.

Blackpool had a decent-sized mob out but it's easy to draw big numbers for an important game. The teams that impressed us were the ones that would turn out in force when we weren't even playing them. Everton were good for that, as were United, much as it pains me to admit it. And then there were the Yids. They were fucking ruthless. Whenever we were in London, they'd be there, ready to have it. If United and Everton were our two main rivals in the north-west then Tottenham were definitely our biggest rivals in the south. They've got a good firm to this day and the lads that were involved when I was on the scene were fucking animals.

They had some proper naughty people and they loved to fight as much as we did.

17

YIDS AND GOONERS

Tottenham's Yid Army never came to City but they were always waiting for us when we travelled down south. They were a godsend when we were playing somebody shit like Charlton, who wouldn't say boo to a goose. We got the train down there safe in the knowledge that they'd be waiting for us at Euston, ready to show us that the whole of London was their manor and that we couldn't just waltz in and out. They didn't give a fuck who we were playing. We were in their city, so we were going to get aggro. They weren't going to let us leave without a fight.

Our friendship with Arsenal didn't exactly help the situation either. It started when a couple of our lads met up with the Gooners in London in 1983 and we offered to go with them to their game against United. It was a proper bonding experience. We spent the whole time picking their brains about their run-ins with the other firms from their neck of the woods and we ended up forming an enduring friendship.

Arsenal's mob told us the best way to get to White Hart Lane without getting ambushed and clued us up on the pubs the Yids drank at and the places they would meet. In return, we told them everything there was to know about the northern firms we'd come up against. They were a proper decent set of lads and I was particularly friendly with a fella called Corbit, who was one of their top geezers. He was one of the gamest people I've had the pleasure of knowing, someone who would never turn his back on you.

I'll never forget the time that Corbit ran headlong into a hefty mob of Tottenham, despite the fact that the rest of our firm were still a good hundred yards down the road. We'd just played Arsenal in a midweek game, in November 1985, and they told us that Spurs would be fronting up at Euston. Not wanting to miss out on a potential ruck, the Gooners offered to join up with us and take on the Yids. Me and Corbit had gone on ahead and the other fifty or so City and Arsenal had fallen slightly behind, meaning we'd be on our own for a good few minutes if we were attacked. We were in a vulnerable position but neither of us gave it a second thought. We were itching to get stuck into Spurs and we weren't afraid to be the first ones into the fray.

Corbit was five eight and looked like a miniature version of Frankenstein. He had a flat, pushed-in face, straight hair and a perfectly square head. He was a proper character, as Cockney as they come. He didn't give a fuck about anything or anyone. The minute he saw Tottenham coming down the road, his eyes lit up. He turned to face me, the excitement written all over his face.

'Right then, oi fackin' 'ate Spurs,' he told me. 'Get yourself over to that skip and find some tools.'

The next thing I knew, Corbit was running towards Tottenham, brandishing an iron bar, an evil glint in his eye. I was right behind. I wasn't going to let him take on their entire firm single-handedly. The fact that Corbit and I had been the first two lads to enter the mêlée cemented our bond and confirmed a mutual respect. Whether it's one on one, or one on a thousand, you have to get stuck in and show the opposition you aren't afraid. I wasn't going to leave him to get weighed in. The rest of our mob were only a matter of minutes away and I didn't mind taking a bit of a beating in the meantime. We ended up getting the better of Tottenham that day and Arsenal were proper impressed by the way we had fought alongside them.

'I'll tell you what, Man City are the fackin' dog's bollocks,' was Corbit's conclusion, after we had seen the Yids off.

He was always the first to give credit where it was due and it's a shame he's not here to see me giving him credit. A couple of years ago, the police found his body chopped into pieces and scattered across the capital. I don't know why it happened but it's a horrible thing to happen to anyone. He was a true friend and he will be sorely missed by everybody who knew him, regardless of their affiliations.

Teaming up with Arsenal gave us the chance to mix with people we wouldn't have otherwise got to mix with. I can still remember the shock when I asked one of them what he did for a living and he told me that he worked in the stock exchange. I knew that they were rich down south but I didn't expect the wealth to have spread to their hooligans as well. It eventually transpired that he was a runner for one of the London stockbrokers but even that was a couple of steps up the ladder from the jobs that City's firm were doing, which partly consisted of robbing things and selling drugs. The Cockneys had money, we had nothing. Most of us had to rely upon crime to make a living, whereas the Arsenal lads were in full-time employment.

The Gooners may have hailed from a different social background but they were kindred spirits when it came to football. They were always proper up for it and they were even more anti-Tottenham than we were, which meant that they would tip us off whenever the Yids were planning an attack. This proved to be an invaluable asset whenever we were in London. I remember in August 1986 when Tottenham's firm were plotting to leave the game early so that they could ambush us on the way out of the ground. We had a couple of Arsenal lads with us, both of whom were in the know, and one of them was proper shitting himself, thinking we were going to come unstuck.

'You need to leave the match even earlier than they do,' he told us. 'That way you won't be walking straight into an ambush the minute you get outside.'

While some people might have been intimidated by the fact that Tottenham's firm were looking to do us in, I was made up. I was bristling with the intense sense of anticipation children feel on Christmas Eve, knowing that they're going to open their presents in a couple of hours. Football violence was the one thing I had to look forward to during the week and, by the day of the match, I was too excited to be afraid.

'If they want a row, they can have a fucking row,' I told the rest of the firm, ushering them towards the exit. 'Let's go and pay them a visit in their own backyard.'

Instead of going to the left when we came out of the ground, towards Tottenham Court Road tube, we made a beeline for the Broadwater Farm estate, right in the heart of Tottenham's manor. I figured that if we hung about in the middle of their territory it would send a clear message that we were up for it, even though there were only between thirty and forty of us.

Broadwater Farm had a reputation for being a no-go area but it was similar to a lot of the estates I'd knocked about in. It was a moody place but there were areas like that in every town and city. The only thing that made the Farm different from the areas that I was familiar with was that the majority of the residents were black. There were dreadlocked Rastas standing about on the pavements, looking at us suspiciously, as if to say: 'What the bumbaclaat are this lot doing here?'

Truth be told, I felt a lot more comfortable in places like Broadwater Farm than I did in the more upmarket areas of London. The accents may have been different but the essence of the area was the same as in Gorton. It reminded me of the old Brookhouse flats, a notorious council estate that had been demolished a couple of years earlier. Knowing estates like Beswick Fort and Longsight Fort in Manchester, I wasn't fazed by venturing into a so-called no-go area. If anything it was an advantage because it kept us alert, ready for when the Yids showed up.

Just as we thought we'd managed to bowl into the epicentre of their territory completely unopposed, one of our lads came running down the road, yelling at the top of his voice.

'They know where we are. Tottenham are coming. They know which way we've come and they're on their way.'

It was the moment we'd been waiting for.

'Right,' I said, a note of urgency in my voice. 'Let's get tooled up. We need all the help we can get.'

There was a skip around the corner and we armed ourselves with sticks and iron bars and hid behind a wall.

'When they get here, blitz them with everything you've got. If you don't, we're going to get fucking slaughtered,' I told the lads.

By the time Tottenham arrived, we were beside ourselves with excitement. It was dark and we could just about make out our rivals' shadows, silhouetted against the dull night sky.

'We're going to get these fackin' Manc barstards,' one of them proclaimed to his mates. He sounded disconcertingly sure of himself. There were hundreds of them and they must have had us outnumbered at least three to one.

'Look Benny. You're fucking crazy if you do this,' one of the Arsenal boys whispered.

'Look. We're Man City and we're doing it. No doubt about it.' And with that, we let out an almighty cry of 'Guvnooooors!' and ran around the corner, tooled up to fuck and looking to show the Yids that we were ready for anything. Tottenham stopped dead in their tracks and we went tearing into them with sticks, iron bars, bottles and half bricks.

Once it kicks off, you forget about everything else that's going on in your life. You brain goes into autopilot. I've read books by so-called hooligans in which the author describes the fights he has had in perfect detail. That's when you know they're talking out of their fucking arses. When you're caught up in the moment, everything is a blur. You become a slave to your subconscious. Life-and-death decisions are made in the blink of an eye: duck, punch, parry, kick, block, kick, punch. You haven't got time to think, you just do it.

Despite their superior manpower, we soon had the Yids on their toes. They retreated down Tottenham High Street and went into a pub, where they were joined by another fifty of their lads. I couldn't believe how well we were doing. We only had a small firm out and we were proper slapping them.

The action continued all the way to the tube, where the Old Bill managed to close the entrance off just as two-thirds of our firm had piled onto the platforms. This was bad news for the lads who were stranded on the other side of the gate. Now they were even more out-numbered and to make matters worse there was no way of escaping.

After a couple of minutes of intense pummelling at the hands of our good friends the Yids, the dibble reopened the entrance and we were reunited with the missing section of our firm. The Old Bill then frantically attempted to close the gates but Tottenham surged forward and forced their way onto the platform. Now that the Guvnors were back together, it was time to teach the Cockneys another lesson.

The coppers eventually managed to split the two sets of hooligans up and ushered us onto our train. However, despite their best efforts, we were able to get a good couple of minutes of fighting in before they regained control. We completely dominated Tottenham. We fucking embarrassed them. We slapped them silly despite the huge disparity in numbers. It was a result and a half, although the night's festivities had only just begun. We still had to get the train back to Piccadilly from Euston and I had a feeling that we hadn't seen the last of the Yids.

'Well,' I grinned, still proper made up. 'Shall we go for a couple of pints at the Lord and Lamb to celebrate?'

As I've said before, I'm not into the whole drinking thing but the Lord and Lamb was in Somers Town, right in the heart of the Gooners' manor, and we were always made to feel welcome there. It was a home from home.

Somers Town has been notorious for crime and deprivation ever since the mid 1800s, when local journalist John Hollingshead commented that it was 'contributing its share to the general mass of misery' and ranked it amongst the 'worst parts of London'.[24] The edge of the area has undergone significant gentrification over the last couple of decades, what with the constant influx of tourists that pass through there en route to St Pancras. This makes it a shit place to go to. I prefer the pubs towards the centre of the estate, where the Old Bill are afraid to go to and you can spark up a spliff without the locals batting an eyelid. I feel more at home in those places and, besides, I've got to know the landlord at the Lord and Lamb over the years and he opens the pub up for us whenever we're in town.

After a brief drinking session with some of our friends from the estate, we headed over to Euston Road to see if the Yids were there. There was no sign of them when we first arrived but then, at eight o'clock, a hundred-strong mob confidently strode through the entrance, looking for payback. Unfortunately, by the time they reached the platform, the transport police had arrived en masse, ready to unleash their dogs at the first sign of trouble. It would have been the perfect ending to the perfect day if we had leathered the Cockneys again but we were left to hurl abuse at them from behind an impenetrable wall of coppers. It was a shame because some of the run-ins that we've had with the Yids at Euston have been fucking unbelievable. Once again, the Old Bill had ruined our fun.

Despite being deprived of the chance to leather them for the second

---

[24] Hollingshead, John: *Ragged in London*, published in 1861.

time, I couldn't help feeling we'd done ourselves proud. Not only had we got the better of one of our closest rivals but we'd also done it with a fraction of our usual numbers, and with a relatively young mob. It must have been humiliating for them to know that fifty City had chased a hundred and fifty of them across the city like a dog chasing a rabbit.

It's not the only time we've triumphed against the odds where Spurs are concerned. In October 1985 a massive mob of Tottenham ambushed seven of us in London, when we were on the way back from a game against Watford. Browny, one of the main Yids, had lied to the rest of the firm, telling them that we'd taken liberties with him. They had then set out to find us, incensed at our supposed deviation from the unwritten code of honour that every self-respecting hooligan abides by.

Browny liked to exaggerate so that he could spur his fellow Yids into action. It later transpired that he had ripped his shirt, ruffled his hair and ran into Tottenham's boozer, telling them that we'd ambushed him at Euston Road and battered him while he was on his own, waiting for a train.

'There were fucking hundreds of them,' he lied, trying his best to look as if he'd taken a brutal beating a couple of minutes earlier. 'Quick, let's get a firm together and haul our arses over to the station so that we can teach those dirty northern bastards a lesson.'

Sure enough, as we were stood at our platform waiting for the train, a huge mob of Tottenham appeared, with Browny leading the way. It was a surprise because we hadn't been expecting trouble. Watford's firm are a fucking joke. Dougie Brimson[25] has forged a career off the back of his time with their so-called Drunk and Disorderly mob but where the fuck were they when we were sat in their seats, abusing them for the full ninety minutes and taking the piss out of them for having Elton John as their chairman? Mr Brimson turns up at book signings and government-led debates on hooliganism but when has anyone ever seen him throw a punch? In my eyes he's a fucking con artist and he

---

[25] The man behind the abomination that was *Green Street*. It's funny how he considers himself to be qualified to dramatise the lives of notorious football hooligans when, to my knowledge, he's never had a single conviction for football-related violence. He's from Watford for fuck's sake. They've got to have the shittest firm in Britain.

doesn't have the slightest clue about our lives. Watford are a firm of no shows and no marks and everybody knows it, but he's going around writing books proudly proclaiming that he was one of their main lads. He really doesn't have a lot going for him.

By complete contrast, Browny and his boys were the real McCoy.

'We're going to fucking do you,' one of the Yids threatened, as Tottenham circled around us like a pack of hungry wolves.

'Yeah, right. Look at your leader. He's just a little funky,' I replied.

'Funky' was a word that we used to describe the type of black lads who hung around at the local shopping centre all day, dressed in weird, baggy clothing and dodgy flowery shirts. They were always bowling around the place, giving it the top-boy walk and trying it on with passing women. We called them 'funkies' because they were into Shalimar [26] and other cheesy disco bands. The thing about Browny was that as well as being a funky he was also a typical scruffy Cockney and the disco look doesn't really work when you've got crumbs around your mouth and frizzy, uncombed Afro-hair sticking out of your head.

'You look a fucking state. Sort yourself out and then maybe we'll take you seriously,' I told him.

Despite my tough talk, I was shitting myself. There was a good chance we were going to get seriously hurt by the time the train arrived.

'Shall I cut him for you?' one of Tottenham's lads asked Browny, reaching into his pocket.

They were geeing themselves up to do something. That much was obvious. Sure enough, a second later, one of them drew his fist back and smacked one of our lads square in the mouth. Rather than exhibit fear, the lad that he had twatted spat a mouthful of blood out into his attacker's face, as if to say, 'Is that all you've got for me? If you're going to fucking stab us then pull your finger out and do it.'

At that point I panicked and, for some unknown reason, grabbed the Yid who had thrown the punch. I dragged him along the ground towards the exit, strangling him as I went.

'Come on then you knobheads,' I yelled, wondering what the fuck

---

[26] An American disco act popular in the 1970s and 1980s.

I was going to do with him once I'd got him to the station doors. 'Come on, outside now. This is what you want, right?'

Was I really offering Tottenham's entire firm out? Had I lost my marbles or was my subconscious hatching a secret escape plan? To my amazement, the seething mass of Yids that stood between me and the exit parted like the Red Sea. I was able to drag my victim across the station completely unopposed.

'Come on. Get him outside,' yelled the Guvnor who had been punched in the mouth, attempting to make out that he was in on whatever it was that I was doing. The rest of the Yids stood around staring at me, as if to say, 'What the fucking hell is going on?'

'Where are you taking him?' one of them piped up, attempting to break the awkward silence.

By this point I was a couple of yards away from the exit and the rest of our mob had come across to join me.

'I'll tell you what I'm fucking doing,' I bellowed and, with that, me and the lad who had spat the mouthful of blood out picked the Yid up and hurled him through the air onto the hard, stone floor.

This was our cue to make a run for it. Tottenham's fallen comrade was positioned conveniently between them and us, giving us just enough time to make a speedy retreat while they checked to see if he was all right. I had been strangling him for a good couple of minutes and he sounded like he was having a fucking asthma attack.

Luckily, the police turned up shortly after we'd gone through the exit and we were able to walk back into the station as if we'd never left it. Tottenham must have thought I was a psycho for offering them all outside like that but I had been acting out of sheer terror.

A couple of minutes later, one of Tottenham's white lads rather tentatively walked over and asked us where the rest of our firm were.

'This is it. There's just us lot. Why, did you think that there were more of us knocking about?' I asked.

The Yid looked puzzled.

'Well, Browny told us that there was a massive mob of you. . .' he started off. He didn't need to finish the sentence. I knew exactly what had happened.

'Oi Browny,' I yelled. 'Get your arse over here. You've got some explaining to do.'

Browny had managed to sneak outside the station like the crafty little Cockney toe rag he is. To his credit, he wasn't actually all that bad a lad, and he could hold his own in a scrap, but what he did that day could have resulted in us getting badly injured. People like him make a hazardous situation twice as bad because if a firm thinks that you've taken liberties with them it pisses them off big time.

I don't take liberties and anyone who has ever had a run-in with me can vouch for that. One on one, or one hundred on one hundred, fair enough, but I would never victimise a lone Tottenham lad, no matter how much of a scruffy, crummy-mouthed funky he was.

Although we've managed to get the better of them a fair few times over the years, Tottenham's firm are still a force to be reckoned with. They've been lucky in a way because they haven't been raided half as much as some of the other Cockney mobs. The police have never been that interested in them for some reason, focussing more on Arsenal, Chelsea and West Ham. That lack of attention from the dibble has enabled them to keep their major players intact, making them a worthy opponent.

If it wasn't for Tottenham, a lot of our trips to the capital would have been uneventful. My only criticism is that they never fronted up at Maine Road. They'd travel to United and Liverpool but yet we only came to blows with them when we were in London. I don't under-stand it. If I was them, I would have relished the opportunity to take us on in our own backyard. Never mind. We could always rely on United for some action back home.

When you share a city with a team that will attack you on sight, you need your wits about you. After a run-in with Spurs, we could relax safe in the knowledge that we would never bump into them in the course of our everyday lives. The Red Army was a different kettle of fish. With them, hooliganism was a 24/7 affair and our rivalry was about to reach a new level of intensity.

It was time for Manchester's notorious Town Wars.

18

THE TOWN WARS

'The Town Wars' is a term used to describe a period of regular mass brawling between ourselves and the Munichs that lasted from the end of one season to the start of the next. Every Friday and Saturday night, we'd meet up in town for a drink. Almost inevitably we would bump into United's mob, usually at three in the morning when we'd been bunged out onto the streets at last orders and were looking for other ways to entertain ourselves. The minute we saw them, all hell would break loose. The Reds can brag and boast, saying that we've never come out on top against them, but actions speak louder than words. We've smashed up so many of their boozers that we've probably kept half the local window fitters in business.

While the Munichs favoured the trendy wine bars on Deansgate, we would be found in the pubs around Oxford Road, taking copious amounts of drugs so that we didn't have to spend as much on beer. United's mob were well off compared to us and they splashed their money around, which made their boozers all the more pleasurable to trash. There's nothing like throwing a brick through an expensive stained-glass window to send a tingle down the curve of your spine.

We'd usually start by bombarding a pub with projectiles to lure the Munichs out. When we did the Sawyers Arms in 1986, United started chucking chair legs out at us so we threw them back. It was a bad move on their part as it provided us with ammunition and it meant that we didn't have to look around for bricks.

Pubs weren't the only properties that got trashed. We demolished a café on the approach to Piccadilly where our rivals were having lunch.

My mate threw a bin through the window and I pelted their firm with pieces of broken glass.

Even when there were no lads drinking in them, boozers would get done over and one of the most memorable episodes from the Town Wars era was the night United smashed up a boozer called the Crown and Kettle, thinking we were trapped inside. In fact we had snuck out of the back door and we were hiding behind billboards, watching them lay into the pub and laughing hysterically.

'They're not in here,' yelled the barmaid, exasperated at their sheer stupidity. 'You're wasting your time. They left ages ago.'

United were bombarding the pub for a good ten minutes before one of them looked through the window and noticed that we had gone. We were fucking pissing ourselves. You would have thought they would have realised what was going on when none of the bricks got chucked back.

The Crown and Kettle, on Oldham Road, has sustained a fair amount of damage over the years. We must have smashed it up at least three times. It was eventually closed for fifteen years in 1989, after a full-scale riot broke out between rival sets of fans on a derby day.[27] If you're running an establishment that has hundreds of drunken revellers coming through its doors every night of the week then trouble comes with the territory. It's impossible to run a pub without fights breaking out.

Destructive as our raids on United's boozers were, it was a street fight in 1987 that led to a marked escalation in our feud. Funnily enough, it didn't involve any of our lads, although we inevitably got the blame from the Munichs. The Cockney Reds had come down from London for the night and one of the Manchester Reds had come running into the pub, announcing that there was a hefty mob of City in one of the nearby boozers. Unfortunately for them, the main United firm had just come out of a different pub and they were walking down the street to take us on. Seeing a massive mob of Mancs striding towards them, the Cockneys automatically assumed it was the Guvnors and a pitched battle ensued between the two sets of Reds.

---

[27] They had rather foolishly offered reduced-price doubles on a day when City were playing United, big mistake.

During the commotion, one of the Mancunian Munichs tripped and fell and a baying pack of Cockney Reds jumped on top of him and beat him mercilessly. The poor cunt took so much punishment that he ended up in a coma. Unwilling to admit that they had hospitalised a member of their own firm, United pointed the finger. They claimed that we were responsible for what happened to their mate. I was insistent from the start that we had nothing to do with it but they were convinced we'd taken liberties. Rumours started flying and there was talk of high-ranking United lads coming after us with shooters. Our rivalry had escalated to the point where nothing was out of bounds. They were hell-bent on revenge and for whatever reason somebody had decided to throw my name into the mix, just to spice things up a bit.

There were a lot of stupid stories doing the rounds about me. Wannabe hooligans were dropping me into their conversations in an attempt to big themselves up and it was causing me no end of trouble. The funny thing was that half of them swore I was black when they were describing me. There were even rumours going around that I was six-foot tall, which couldn't have been further from the truth. Did they think that the name 'Little Benny' was ironic? I would have to prove to the Munichs that I didn't take liberties. Several of our firm had received unexpected visits at their houses and things were getting out of hand.

The opportunity to prove myself came on the way back from a pre-season friendly against Wrexham. We were dropping a lad called Eli[28] off at his house in Bury when he took it upon himself to invite the whole firm in while his mum and dad were away on holiday. Eli's brother was a well-known Red Army member and it was an offer we couldn't refuse.

'He'll be in bed at this time,' Eli grinned. 'He'll get the shock of his life when he sees you lot stood about the house.'

'Right here's what we're going to do,' I told the rest of the firm, making sure that they all knew the score. 'We're going to wake him

---

[28] Eli's another person who doesn't appear on the list of firm members. A lot of people respect his older brother, who is a United lad, but Young Eli is an embarrassment, end of. More about that later.

up and show him we can go round to their houses, just like they can go round to ours. Nobody is to lay a fucking finger on him though. Do you hear me?'

They nodded in agreement. The plan was to show him that we could have done him if we wanted to but that we weren't the type of people who would take advantage of someone in a vulnerable position. It was the perfect way to demonstrate to the Munichs that we could escalate the situation even further than they could but that we were unwilling to do so, as we didn't want to stoop to their level.

Everything would have gone according to plan but someone in our ranks had sticky fingers. One of the lads nicked a sovereign ring from Eli's brother's dressing table, which enraged the Red Army even more when they got wind of it. As far as United were concerned, the theft constituted another liberty. I tried to explain to them that it wasn't what we had planned but it fell on deaf ears. Our lad shouldn't have taken the ring but the Munichs shouldn't have falsely accused us of doing their mate. It was a case of six of one, half a dozen of the other. They should have saved the violence for when both sides were both mobbed up rather than targeting individual members of our firm in pointless acts of vengeance.

There were a number of tit-for-tat attacks during the Town Wars period, most of them below the belt. One such incident occurred when two of United's lads, Mook and Gilbert, came sidling up to me and Spinner in town, asking who our least favourite members of their firm were.

'Oh it's got to be that wanker Mook,' I smirked. 'He's a right bent bastard.' Mook was an openly gay hooligan. He wasn't the in-your-face, acting-like-a-woman type of gay but, at the same time, he was never one to hide his sexuality and I suppose you can't fault him for that. We took the piss but he wasn't arsed what anybody said. He was happy with who he was.

'You cheeky little bastard,' Mook exclaimed, and, with that, he banged Spinner hard in the mouth, proving that homosexuals aren't all sissies like the media make them out to be. Mook was a proper game lad and his sexuality was neither here nor there. He could hold his own in a fight and that was the only thing that mattered to us.

A brief scuffle ensued, resulting in Gilbert getting slashed across the arse with a Stanley knife and Mook doing a runner. Gilbert was from Wythenshawe, where I was living at the time, and I shouldn't have let him get a blade in him but it was hard to avoid. In the heat of the moment, it's easy to end up doing things that are out of order. Although saying that, a couple of weeks earlier, he had battered me round the head with a pool cue and lobbed a load of snooker balls at me. When you're fighting with rival hooligans, day in, day out, you've got to expect to take one every now and again.

If it was the other way round, I would have taken the slashing in my stride but people react to these things in different ways. Gilbert saw it as the ultimate act of disrespect and he was determined to have it out with me. So, the following day, the Munichs asked a Wythenshawe lad called Stoner where I lived. They were planning on turning up at my gaff, armed with baseball bats, but Stoner didn't want to drop me in it so he took them to the wrong address. If he'd have taken them to my house he could have landed me in serious trouble. There was a rumour going round that one of Gilbert's entourage was looking to put a gun to my head, which could have ended up with me in a body bag.

A couple of days later, Gilbert turned up at Spinner's gaff, running his mouth off, telling him that he was going to weigh me in the next time he saw me.

'I've got a message for your mate Benny. Let him know that when I get my hands on him, I'm going to do him over good and proper. It's going to be a hospital job.'

As it happened, I was round at Spinner's house at the time and I was listening in on the conversation, itching to explain my side of the story to the poor misguided Munich.

'Tell him yourself,' Spinner replied. 'He's in the other room. I'll get him for you.'

'Yeah, tell me yourself,' I piped up, poking my head round the door. 'What are you going on like this for? Getting slashed is nothing. At the end of the day, I'm four foot and you're six foot. In a situation like that, we're going to use any means necessary to get the upper hand. It may not have been the right thing to do but it's not as if we planned it that way. It just happened.'

Gilbert paused for a second, as if he was taking a moment to view the situation from our perspective.

'Okay,' he told me, 'I can accept that.'

I hadn't finished yet.

'And what about you coming round here, doing this?'

I wasn't the only one who had done something out of order. It takes two to tango. I wanted him to acknowledge that he was just as bad as us.

'I heard that you were trying to find out where I lived the other day as well,' I added, hammering home his previous failed attempt to get at me.

'No, no, no; you've got it all wrong. I stopped the lads from coming round here. They're round the corner and they're tooled up. But I've told them to stay where they are unless you try any funny business. I wanted to see what you had to say before I got anybody else involved,' Gilbert explained.

I wasn't sure if he was bluffing so I decided to test whether there really was anybody else to back him up, or whether he was making it up so that I'd think he'd done me a favour by coming to the door on his own.

'Well you'd better go and get them. There's no point leaving them round there,' I told him.

'Nah, there's no need now,' Gilbert replied, a lot more relaxed about the situation now that I had explained the motivation behind the slashing. 'I'll go and tell them there's nobody home.'

I never did find out whether there was anybody there but Gilbert was a trustworthy lad so I think he was telling the truth. It's funny because I became really good mates with him, despite him being a Munich and despite us being embroiled in such a bitter feud. We ended up working the in-out at the local pop concerts together and he turned out to be a loyal and genuine lad once I'd got to know him.

Unfortunately, Gilbert managed to get himself addicted to gear a couple of years down the line and he's sadly no longer with us. His lifeless body was found in his flat several weeks after he died, chock full of heroin and slowly decomposing. Nobody had been to see him since before the day of his overdose. I had tears in my eyes when I found out. What a horrible way to go.

Gilbert and Mook were both proper decent lads. You're probably thinking 'How can you say that about them after you were involved in an incident where one of them got slashed?' Well he had a scar on his arse and that was it. We wouldn't have done his face. I would have done a Scouser in the face but not somebody I knew and, to be fair, probably not a United lad. I was genuinely remorseful that Gilbert ended up getting a stripe but, if he had been carrying the knife, he would have done the same thing to me and I wouldn't have held it against him. In the heat of battle, you've got no time to think. The moment you realise the blade is in your pocket, you whip it out and cut someone. I am sorry Gilbert was on the receiving end but it was unavoidable.

Strangely enough, I became good friends with Mook. He may have been as bent as a nine-bob note but he was always up for a fight and he was a really likeable fella once I got past the fact that he was queer. He was gangster number one in Salford and he was always double generous with his money, one of the reasons that United could afford to drink in their trendy Deansgate boozers every Friday and Saturday night. He made it a matter of principle to provide for the rest of his firm and he was one of the soundest people you could meet.

Embarrassingly for us, it was a City fan who brought it on top for Mook. Mook was one of Salford's top armed blaggers. He had been doing Bradford and Bingley branches over week in, week out for as long as I could remember and he could have carried on doing them, had he not brought in a closet-gay City lad. Although Mook invariably worked alone, on this occasion he made an exception. He took Eli, his latest fling, round to the building society and showed him how to rob the place.

'If you get into any trouble, I'll come in and rescue you,' he had told him. 'Right, put your bally down and go and get your money.'

The graft ended up going off without a hitch and they got away with a hundred and sixty grand. Mook took his mates abroad with his share, making sure they didn't have to spend a penny for the entire holiday. While they were living it up in a five-star hotel, Eli's bird had somehow got wind of what he'd been up to. She demanded to know if it was true that he was cheating on her with another man. Rather than doing the honourable thing and coming clean to her about his sexuality, the dirty grassing bastard decided to bubble to the Five-O so that Mook would end up getting put away until the rumours had subsided. That way he could be sure that his homosexual lover couldn't spill the beans about their gay affair.

Eli went to the Old Bill and told them about every last Bradford and Bingley that Mook had done, including the one they carried out as a joint venture. What a fucking snake! It's not as if we would have cared that much that he was bent. We'd have given him stick but that would've been it. He ended up getting off with community service, a fucking disgrace if you ask me. It just goes to show what you can get away with if you're willing to put someone in the frame.

Mook ended up doing a twelve-year stint and, as luck would have it, he was sent to Strangeways, where I was serving a sentence for violent disorder. I can still remember the first time I saw him walking along the landings. I thought, 'fucking hell, here comes trouble'. Luckily, he was willing to let bygones be bygones and he greeted me with a friendly handshake, rather than the swift blow to the head I was expecting.

'It's a shame we didn't meet under different circumstances. You know the score in here though, don't you Benny? We're all on the same side. It's not City versus United, it's cons versus screws.'

I was impressed by Mook's diplomatic outlook. He was similar to me. He was willing to look past a person's football affiliations and see them for who they really were. Once I got to know him and we started hanging out together on the landings, he asked me to get a message out to the rest of his firm, letting them know the score about that snaky fucker Eli. He couldn't get the message out himself, as his visitors were being closely monitored.

'Our lads need to know the truth,' he said. 'You never know who else he's been telling tales on.'

He didn't need to ask me twice. Nobody likes an informer and I had no qualms about blowing the whistle on the filthy grassing cunt to United's mob.

'Don't worry about it. I'll sort it for you. I'll put the word out on my visit next week,' I assured him.

Although I had every intention of getting Mook's message out to United's firm, it proved easier said than done, as none of my visitors would have anything to do with it.

'He's a United lad. I'm not passing anything on for him,' they insisted.

I tried to explain that it transcended football allegiances but they stuck to their guns.

'They're not carrying on like that, are they?' sighed Mook, taken aback by the depth of feeling between United and City. 'Look I'll show you my depositions if you want. They prove I was grassed up.'

He didn't need to prove anything to me. It was just frustrating that I couldn't do more to help him. I felt we were partly responsible for what had happened to him, seeing as it was one of our lads who had grassed.

'Don't worry,' I told him, 'I'll make sure everybody knows the score. I'll teach the bastard a lesson for you as well. Leave it with me and I'll have him kidnapped.'

As it turned out, United's firm were more than capable of sorting Eli out on their own and a couple of weeks down the line, one of their lads got caught driving to the fucker's house with a shotgun in the back of his car. Anybody who knows the fella knows full well that he would have shot the grassing prick if the coppers hadn't pulled him over when they did. He ended up getting eighteen months for possession of a firearm and the fact that he was willing to risk a murder charge to even up the score for his friend shows the loyalty that being in a mob breeds.

Eli disappeared, never to be seen again. He's still alive but he's keeping a low profile and he should count himself lucky that he hasn't ended up six feet under. Mook had powerful allies. He wasn't the type that you could bubble on; there would be recriminations. He was well connected across the country, one of Salford's top-tier criminals. Within a year of getting out of Strangeways, he was caught smuggling a kilo of coke out of Thailand and he eventually died in a Thai prison under mysterious circumstances. Some say he had a heart attack; others claim that he was murdered by the guards during an escape attempt. Whatever happened, he was a proper game lad and he is sorely missed. There weren't too many high-ranking villains who shared the wealth around to the extent that he did. He was always lavishing his riches on the other United lads and he did the same with me in jail.

R.I.P. Mook. You were respected by City and United alike. You may have been a crook, but you were a crook with a heart of gold.

I've got to give the Munichs credit where it's due. They had a lot of serious career criminals: smugglers, blaggers, dealers, burglars, fraudsters; you name it. We were a ragtag bunch of thieves; they were the crème de la crème. Lads like Mook took what we were doing to another level. City were selling drugs and doing the odd post-office robbery but United were getting their drugs straight from the Colombians and doing over banks and building societies on a weekly basis. Their connection to the Cockney Reds meant they were able to network with the top grafters from down south. While we were busy stealing designer clothing from the stores during spur-of-the-moment shoplifting expeditions, they were planning international drug-smuggling operations and sitting down with major crime lords.

My friendship with Mook forced me to develop a grudging respect for the Munichs. Not only were they good at what they did but they also had some proper honourable lads. They were mostly criminals but they weren't the types of criminals who went out mugging old ladies. They were decent, honest crooks, if that isn't a contradiction in terms. They may have chosen a money-hungry team to support but if you've got money to spare then I suppose you might as well spend it following a club that charges exorbitant prices for its tickets.

We may not have had as many serious criminals in our firm but we had our fair share of hard cases. It doesn't take a big-time gangster to cut somebody open. It takes a man with a major grudge and one of City's older lads, who I shall refer to as 'Garry', decided to prove that point.

It was just my luck to have been at the scene of the crime.

19
WRONG PLACE, WRONG TIME

Garry was ten years older than me and he'd been going to the football since the Sixties. He lived in Moston, an area notorious for organised crime, and most of the residents knew not to cross him, although it just so happened that I was a couple of streets down from him on my way to buy a pint of milk on the day when he decided to settle a violent feud that had been brewing for some time.

I have a nasty habit of being in the wrong place at the wrong time and this was no exception. I was walking to the newsagent when Daft Donald came bounding over towards me with a smile spread across his face, eager to embroil me in his latest craziness.

'I don't know where you're heading but fuck it off. It's all going off, Benny. It's proper going off,' he said excitedly.

What was he on about? As far as I knew, there was nobody turning out for us that day. We had just played West Brom but they hadn't brought a mob with them.

'Some of the lads are in the pub round the corner. They're off to Moston. I'm telling you, it's going off big time there.'

At the time I assumed they'd arranged a meeting with United, who must have been in Moston, waiting for us. My friendship with Mook may have diluted the hatred I felt towards the Reds but it hadn't lessened my enthusiasm for scrapping with them. I hadn't had a decent run-in with the Munichs for a while and I was eager to get stuck in.

'Count me in. I'll pick the milk up on my way back home.'

I arrived at the pub just as a group of the Guvnors' naughtiest lads were leaving.

'Quick, get in. We need a proper little mob for a show of strength,' I was told.

Well that was stating the fucking obvious, because that was always the case when we were having it with the Munichs.

As the car pulled into a quiet residential street on Moston's Mill estate, I felt a tight knot of tension forming in my stomach. Something wasn't right. I couldn't see any United.

'I'm not into this,' one of my mates piped up, cutting through the awkward silence.

'Not into what?' I asked him.

By this stage I knew we hadn't turned out for the Munichs. The lads had a look of steely determination on their faces and, whatever they'd come to do, it wasn't anything to do with football.

'I'm not into going into people's houses,' he went on. 'I just don't agree with it. I'm staying out here. You can count me out.'

'Yeah I'm staying here as well. I didn't know that we were going round to somebody's gaff. I don't want anything to do with it,' I agreed.

A couple of the other lads were of the same mind and we waited outside in the car while Garry and his boys ballied up and piled into a house, looking ready for trouble.

'I don't even want to stick about. I'll do a three-point turn and we can fuck off home and meet up with the rest of the firm later,' the driver said.

I felt the same way. Whatever was about to go off had nothing to do with us. It was between Garry and the owner of the house. There was no need for us to be there.

Just as the car was pulling out of the estate, I heard a sudden scream of 'open the doors' and I saw a group of agitated-looking Guvnors running along the pavement towards us.

'Quick! Open the fucking doors,' yelled someone who shall remain nameless.

I did as he said and, the next thing I knew, one of our younger lads had flung himself onto the back seat. He was gibbering about someone getting stabbed.

'What's the deal with him?' I asked Garry.

'Never mind him. We need to get the fuck out of here, double quick.' His face was bright red. He was buzzing about something.

At the time, I assumed that the talk about blades and people getting cut was the product of an overactive imagination. Surely they wouldn't have needed us there for back up if they were planning on stabbing someone. Going round to people's houses and slicing them open wasn't the type of thing the Guvnors were known for either. We were into street fights and pub brawls, not sticking a chiv into somebody while they were at home relaxing. It was only when we parked up at one of the lads' houses and whacked the Teletext on that I found out what had happened.

'Cold-blooded gang killing in Moston,' read the headline.

Fuck me, this wasn't good.

'Thirty men in balaclavas entered the house, while their accomplices blocked the road off in their car to stop the other residents from intervening,' the report said.

Eh? That was us. And we were doing a three-point turn, we weren't blocking off the road. They were making it sound like something out of *The Sopranos*.

'This is fucking unreal,' I said to Frankie. 'We're going to get life over this.'

By this stage, somebody had switched the channel over to the news and a reporter was going on about what a brutal murder it had been.

'How can an assassination like that happen in this day and age?' she asked the viewers. 'It was a killing in broad daylight and the police believe that the people responsible were violent football hooligans, associated with Manchester City Football Club's Young Guvnors gang.'

Fuck. This definitely wasn't good.

'They are looking out for three males in their early twenties, two Caucasian and one Afro-Caribbean, who were seen driving away from the scene of the crime in a dark-coloured saloon car.'

The entire world was conspiring against me. I'd gone out for a pint of milk and here I was being accused of murder.

It later transpired that Garry had put a pair of gloves and a balaclava on shortly after entering the house. He then pinned his victim to the wall while he calmly plunged a knife into his heart. We could have ended up getting the blame but, fortunately, one of the lads had a crisis of conscience and grassed Garry up to the coppers. If Garry hadn't been put in the frame who knows what the dibble would have believed. After all, according to them, we'd blocked the street off so that nobody could step in to save the victim.

I could have spent the rest of my life behind bars for something I played no part in.

Garry got ten years for manslaughter, despite the prosecution arguing that 'a more cold-blooded murder would be difficult to imagine'. He got off lightly, all things considered. Garry's defence was that he'd only intended to injure his victim. But, then again, he ended up dying behind bars so I suppose it didn't matter what sentence the judge handed down. Some say he had a heart attack, others claim he took a fatal overdose. Whatever the circumstances, I'd always thought of him as a decent lad up to that point. I was sorry to see him go.

R.I.P. Garry and R.I.P. to his victim as well. I didn't know the lad who was killed personally but I'm sure he hadn't done anything that justified being stabbed to death. He wasn't a rival hooligan and I've been told that the feud started when he scratched a mirror in Garry's house. It's amazing how a little thing like that can develop into something so serious.

The murder was pretty worrying for us. I was even hauled down to the station and interviewed, although they let me go as soon as I'd answered their questions. They must have been satisfied that I had nothing to do with it. We're not a death squad; we're a group of football hooligans. Going round to people's houses over personal disputes is strictly against the rules. If I'd have known what I was getting myself embroiled in, I would have stayed well away. I came within a gnat's whiskers of spending the rest of my life behind bars. It would have been just my luck if I'd been sent down for something that somebody else had done.

Keeping my nose clean is easier said than done. Most of my close friends are habitual lawbreakers and sometimes they will commit harmless acts of illegality, whereas with others it can get extremely naughty. Saying that though, if it wasn't for the football then God only knows what we would be getting up to. It helped us channel our aggression without the need for cutting people up over every little disagreement. Rich people can turn to fox hunting to indulge their violent side. We can't. But then again, we don't need a horse and a pack of dogs to help us hunt our prey. Bricks and bottles are our weapons of choice and they are ten a penny. When there are people getting killed over a scratch on a mirror a bit of fighting at a football match is the least of society's worries.

When you've got your Millwalls and your Tottenhams down south, your Birminghams and your Coventrys in the Midlands and clubs like United and Everton in the north-west, you don't need to burst into people's houses to get your fill of violence. And then there's the Geordies, who are a different kettle of fish altogether. They wear shorts and T-shirts in the depths of winter and they're born with a bottle of Newcastle Brown Ale in their hands. The north-east was a great place to go.

We never left without a ruck.

20

THE NORTH-EAST

It is little wonder that Newcastle is such a stronghold of football hooliganism; even the women are hard round those parts. The Geordies remind me of the Scousers. They've got the same rough-and-ready attitude and the only thing that sets them apart from their Liverpudlian cousins is their fashion sense. They copy the latest trend from Merseyside just as it's on its way out. But what they lack in style they make up for in their willingness to have a scrap. The Newcastle firm, the Gremlins, were always proper up for it whenever we crossed their path and they made the three-hour trip from Manchester well worth the journey. They may have talked like they were recovering from a stroke but they could certainly hold their own.

I've always admired the Gremlins. They're attached to a shit club but they can draw huge numbers. We should have taken the whole firm when we went up against them but things don't always work out like that. When we had our most successful run-in with them, on 26 April 1986, we only had fifteen frontline lads. We had another fifteen borderline hooligans tagging along but we couldn't rely on them when it kicked off. I didn't think we'd be able to take on Newcastle with only a handful of proper lads.

The Old Bill did nothing to ease our nerves. They spent the entire train journey down there winding us up and telling us how badly the Geordies were going to do us.

'You haven't got a very good turnout, have you lads?' Officer Dibble jeered. 'And you know what the Geordies are like.'

I didn't want him to see that he was getting to me so I didn't rise to the bait.

'Yeah. We know what the Geordies are like.'

And with that, I carried on surreptitiously sniffing the poppers one of the lads had given to me, using the rush to mask the feelings of apprehension that were buzzing around my brain. You've got to be willing to take the rough with the smooth. You can't always turn up with a massive entourage. Sometimes you have to grit your teeth and make the best of it.

'It's an open station. They'll be on you the minute you get off the train,' the Old Bill carried on.

I don't know why the copper thought we'd be fazed by the fact that the station didn't have ticket barriers. It just meant there was nothing to stop us from bowling off the platform without paying for our journey. As it happened, he was wrong about the Gremlins being there. We were able to walk straight out of the exit completely unopposed.

The Geordies were plotted up in a Yates's boozer directly to our right as we came out of the station. They had a couple of younger lads but it was mostly beer-bellied, scruffy throwbacks to the 1960s, dressed in proper old-fashioned clothes. As we entered their line of vision, a hundred-strong mob came storming out of the pub. They were armed with bottles and pint glasses, ready to wrap them around our faces.

'Come on lads. We'll show these Geordie wankers what we came here to do,' I shouted.

We somehow managed to chase the entire mob of Gremlins up to the top of the road within a couple of minutes of it going off. They were surprised we had stood our ground. They must have thought, 'Fuck this. There are a hundred of us but only thirty of them. They must have some proper handy lads.' Our winning streak didn't last long though because, in the blink of an eye, the Geordies managed to chase us all the way back down the street.

Not only were we vastly outnumbered but we also had an injured lad in our ranks. Lee Skelly had broken his ankle during a scrap with the Yids and he was hobbling about on crutches. It made him an easy target for the Gremlins and one of their lads chucked a scaffolding pole at him as he struggled to get away. Luckily for Skelly, the Geordie could hardly get the pole off the floor and it only travelled a couple of inches, making him the laughing stock of his entire firm.

Hearing the commotion, the coppers were soon on the scene, trying to put a stop to things.

'Benny,' shouted the officer who had been taunting us on the train a couple of hours earlier. He wasn't so fucking sure of himself now.

'Stop what you're doing right now,' he bellowed.

'I'll tell you what. It's a fucking good job we had a poor turn out today, isn't it? If we had our whole mob with us, think what it would have been like,' I replied, rather smugly.

The Old Bill eventually managed to get the situation under control. They forced us into the back of a police van and drove us to the ground. It was nice of them to give us a lift. Who says that all coppers are wankers?

I can't remember anything about the game, apart from the fact we lost 1–0. Once again, the events on the pitch were a secondary consideration.

As soon as the final whistle had blown, the coppers were on us. They escorted us back to the station and then hung about to make sure we got on our train. We were disappointed that we weren't going to get another pop at the Gremlins but my disappointment quickly converted into excitement when I realised that there were a couple of Newcastle lads in the next carriage. Unfortunately, there was also a line of BTP separating us from them. We tried our hardest to break through the line of Old Bill but to no avail.

Most of the Gremlins left the train at Durham, which seemed to be where the majority of them came from. We'd been unscrewing the light bulbs all journey long and we immediately started lobbing them out of the windows the minute they got onto the platform. The next thing we knew, they were throwing them straight back up at us. Chucking a load of light bulbs around was a poor alternative to a proper row. I would have loved to have disembarked and run them ragged all over Durham but it wasn't to be.

* * *

Although Newcastle is by far the largest city in the north-east, there was another firm from round those parts that could give the Guvnors a run for their money. Middlesbrough's Frontline had some proper hard cases on board and they could pull decent numbers. They were like a smarter, better-dressed version of the Geordies and for a team of their size, they couldn't half have a fight.

We've only had a couple of run-ins with the Frontline over the years because they've usually been in a different division but, every time our paths have crossed, there's been trouble. We played them in the League Cup semi-final in January 1976 and it went off proper so by the time I came to travel up there in 1986, I knew they were no mugs. This time we had a decent mob of between seventy and a hundred. We were looking forward to finding out if Middlesbrough's firm could live up to the hype that surrounded them.

Rather than head straight to Boro, we got the train to Eaglescliffe so that we could avoid getting put into an escort by the Old Bill. Eaglescliffe is a godforsaken little place. There's a nondescript boozer and a rundown train station with graffiti-plastered walls and that's your lot. It reminded me of Miles Platting in Manchester in that there wasn't even a proper parade of shops. Still, it was free of dibble, which made it the perfect place for us to get off.

Donald Francis and the rest of the firm were travelling down to Eaglescliffe in a minivan and we were meant to be meeting them there but we decided to press on to Middlesbrough, rather than wait around for them. We were eager to get stuck into the Frontline.

We arrived in Middlesbrough at one o'clock and set off through the main shopping area towards Ayresome Park. Boro has a small town centre and we had soon come out of the other side into a rough looking council estate. The further we got from the station, the bleaker our surroundings became and the more uneasy I became. Youngish lads in Sergio Tacchini tracksuits were hanging about, giving us the eyeball and attempting to intimidate us as we marched past.

'Keep going, lads,' one of them sneered at me in his funny little accent, a cross between Yorkshire and Geordie, two of the world's most backwards dialects.

'Keep going? We go where the fuck we want,' I scoffed.

As we carried on walking, a horde of Middlesbrough piled out of a dilapidated boozer and came up the hill to meet us. Some were fully fledged hooligans but a lot of them were random nutcases from the local area.

It was the moment we'd been waiting for.

'Let's have you then,' I shouted, as I armed myself with a house brick, ready to smash it into some poor cunt's face.

The rest of the firm followed suit and, before we knew it, we had forced the Frontline and their hangers-on back inside the pub. They were chucking barstools through the doors in a vain attempt to back us off. I was in my fucking element.

The local coppers were quick to intervene and within a couple of minutes, they had shepherded us to the other side of the road. Little did they know that a two hundred and fifty-strong mob of Middlesbrough was waiting for us further along the street. This time they were 100 per cent purebred hooligans, immaculately turned out and ready for war.

The notorious Frontline were a sight to behold. They were dressed in Sergio Tacchini tops and faded jeans and, for some unknown reason, they all had curly hair. A lot of them looked as if they were on steroids. They had big, thick, muscular arms and legs; they were built like brick shithouses.

'Here they come,' one of their top geezers calmly announced. They were disciplined, making sure they stayed in position, content to wait for us to come to them.

By this stage, the majority of our firm had tailed off in different directions looking for the ground. We only had thirty lads left. We did our best to hold our own against the Frontline but it was clear from the start that we were fighting a losing battle. One of the Middlesbrough supporters whacked me in the face with a Millwall brick while the rest of them set about us with keys and belt buckles, revelling in their superior numbers. They beat the shit out of us.

The police were proper on it and they quickly got the situation under control and herded us into the stadium.

'I haven't even got a ticket,' I protested, wanting to stay outside and carry on fighting with Middlesbrough.

'Don't worry. I won't leave you out here to get mullered,' one of the coppers assured me, ushering me towards the turnstiles. 'You'll have to jump over into the stands. You'll get killed if you stay here.'

I remember thinking that the Old Bill had grossly underestimated my ability to defend myself but at the same time feeling pretty made up that I was going to see the game for free.

'Well okay then. If you insist,' I replied.

A fight with two different sets of Boro and now the coppers were letting us into the ground without paying. It was turning out to be a day to remember.

We lost the game 1–0 and all I can remember about the match is that Donald Francis arrived shortly after kick off only for a horde of angry Frontline to smash his minivan to smithereens the minute he parked up. They left it in such a state that the Old Bill had to have it towed away during the game. Donald was fucking fuming, as were the twenty other City lads who had travelled down with him. They were determined to even the score as soon as the final whistle had blown.

Now that we had an extra set of Guvnors on board, I felt we had a better chance. Ayrsome Park is similar to Maine Road. It's surrounded by a maze of terraced streets and if you don't know your way around you can easily come unstuck. It's not an area you'd want to get lost in but, unfortunately for us, that was exactly what happened.

As we ventured further from the ground, our lads started wandering off in different directions. It soon got to the point where there were only forty of us left and, just as we were getting our bearings, a seething mass of Middlesbrough appeared on the horizon, storming along the road. Fuck! There were hundreds of the cunts; we had no chance.

'Arm yourselves,' I told the rest of the mob.

We needed all the help we could get if we were going to make it back to the station without being beaten to a pulp. My instructions paid off. We were able to prevent the Frontline from catching up with us by continuously pelting them with bricks until we'd reached the town centre.

Workmen were carrying out road works on the street leading to the station so we quickly tooled ourselves up with whatever we could get our hands on. There was an assortment of pickaxes and iron bars lying around so we snatched them up and immediately started laying into Middlesbrough. There was nowhere to run and we had no other option but to make a final stand.

There's a big difference between the makeshift weapons you will find in a skip and tools that are designed for hacking big, fuck-off chunks of concrete out of the ground so the odds were now stacked firmly in our favour. Before I knew it, people were getting twatted with traffic cones and pickaxe handles, while I managed to hit one of their lads with a four-foot metal pole with a hook on the end. I was swinging it around all over the shop while the rest of the firm were pelting our rivals with chunks of rubble. We would have done some serious damage if the coppers hadn't promptly arrived.

Once it was over, the Frontline came over to congratulate us.

'Well done lads,' one of them said, extending his hand in my direction. 'You're only young 'uns but you've done all right. You've got a canny good firm.'

Middlesbrough's main geezer was a black fella with a Fila top and thick suede gloves on. He was on the same train as us on the journey back to Piccadilly and he didn't seem fazed by being surrounded by the lads he'd been having it with minutes earlier.

'I'm not causing trouble but here I am,' he proclaimed.

We looked at one another in complete confusion, wondering what to make of him. He was a madhead but I respected him for his bravery. There's a thin line between being a game cunt and being a fucking lunatic and he managed to straddle it very skilfully. I heard he was recently stabbed to death during a street fight so that's yet another R.I.P. to add to the collection. He had guts and I daresay their firm has lost one of its most valuable members. I've got a lot of admiration for people like that, no matter where their allegiances lie.

Although we had just about managed to get the better of the Frontline, thanks to the conveniently placed road works, they had lived up to their reputation and then some. For a club of their size, they were a bunch of fucking animals. It doesn't take a rocket scientist to work out why Middlesbrough has such a formidable group of hooligans. It's one of the most deprived towns in England and there's fuck all else to do. It is one thing being poor and living in a major city like Manchester or London but it's quite another when you're forced to spend your days holed up somewhere like that. The football is the only thing that keeps them going and the same can be said of another similarly disadvantaged northern town we visited. Sometimes the grimmest places produce the most dedicated hooligans.

The town that I'm referring to is so 'grim' that it even has those four letters at the beginning of its name.

21

GRIMSBY

Grimsby is like Southend, only shitter. You go to places like York and Edinburgh and there are big historical buildings as far as the eye can see. You go to Grimsby and the place is desolate, full of inbreeds and hillbillies. The inhabitants look like they were born with an extra finger on each hand. There's only one reason that anybody would ever be excited about travelling to a place like Grimsby and that's to have a row with the local firm.

The first time we were scheduled to play Grimsby was in April 1985, while we were in the waste land that was division two. I thought they might put up some resistance but I didn't think that they'd have a proper organised mob. They weren't exactly renowned for being at the pinnacle of football violence. In fact they weren't exactly renowned for anything. I was hoping we'd get a decent fight out of them but I never for one minute expected they'd hold their own.

The neighbouring town of Cleethorpes is only a stone's throw from Grimsby so we decided to get off the train a stop early in order to throw the Old Bill off the scent. We had the usual set of faces with us. There was me, Frankie, Chrissie James, Little Spinner, Big Spinner, Anthony Rowan and a couple of others. We'd set off double early so it was still only ten o'clock when we reached Cleethorpes but, bizarrely, ten of our older lads were there already, pissed up to fuck and asleep on a grassy verge at the side of the pavement. They had obviously passed out during the previous night's drinking session.

'Oh, here's the young lot,' murmured one of our beer monsters as we walked across the grass.

This roused a drunken Deano into action and he immediately woke up, burped and grabbed the nearest pedestrian by the scruff of the neck.

'Who's nicked me beer?' he shouted, chinning his bewildered victim and pinning him to the ground. The bloke he had got a hold of had nothing to do with the football. He was just a random geezer who happened to be passing.

The rest of our firm looked on in amazement as Deano clambered on top of the fella and started proper laying into him. Not content with pummelling the poor bastard he dragged him across to the seafront and threw him head first into the water. Luckily, the water was relatively shallow and the fella was able to dry himself off and to beat a hasty retreat before he had anything else done to him.

'If you've not nicked my beer then tell me who has,' Deano bellowed, still 100 per cent convinced somebody had pinched his cans. 'Can't you at least tell me where I can go to buy some more?'

We were laughing our fucking heads off. It was proper tight on the bloke who was on the receiving end but it was impossible to keep a straight face.

'It's not even twelve o'clock yet,' I grinned to Frankie. 'This is going to be a fucking day and a half.'

After spending a couple of hours playing on the arcades and laughing about the morning's events, we decided it was time to go. We headed for the beach and set off for Blundell Park on foot. Grimsby shares a coastline with Cleethorpes and it was only a ten-minute walk from one town to the next but, unbeknown to us, the beach was Grimsby's main stomping ground. Within minutes, a group of attractive-looking women had come running over, asking us if we were there for the football.

'Yeah,' I told them, sensing that they might have been sent over by Grimsby's firm to see if we were the Guvnors. 'We're Man City and who wants to know?'

'Grimsby are over there,' the bird at the front of the group replied, pointing towards a mob of backwards-looking lads a hundred yards away. They weren't as badly dressed as some of the firms we've encountered over the years (Blackburn in particular, who are a load of fucking tramps) but they could have picked a better set of colours. They were turned out in purples and pinks. They looked like they'd modelled their clothes on a packet of Fruit Pastels.

The local womenfolk seemed to be more interested in us than they were in Grimsby's mob. Maybe it was because we weren't dressed like something out of a kaleidoscope!

'You're all right you lot, aren't you?' giggled a pretty little blonde bird with a strong Lincolnshire accent. I wonder how it felt for our rivals to know that their birds were proper into a group of lads who had travelled to their town for the specific purpose of battering them. It couldn't have been particularly pleasurable because they were giving us some right funny looks and one of their main lads was heading across the beach.

Grimsby's top boy was a total fucking weirdo. He was dressed in a pink Benneton jumper and a pair of red sunglasses and he fancied himself as a bit of a comedian, although he was about as funny as cancer.

'All right Jack. I'm back,' he proclaimed, putting on a fake Cockney accent in a lame attempt to come across as wacky. 'It makes sense, doesn't it?' he grinned.

I looked at Chrissie and Chrissie looked at me, as if to say, 'What the fuck is this cunt on about?' It didn't make the slightest bit of sense.

'Are you Jack then, yeah?' Chrissie asked him and, the next thing I knew, 'Jack' had received a swift punch to the jaw and he was spitting a mixture of blood and teeth out into the sand. The rest of Grimsby's mob charged forward and we were almost blinded by the myriad of colours on their tops. They looked like something out of *Joseph and the Amazing Technicolor Dreamcoat*.

We didn't even bother going to the game. I may be a football hooligan but the 'football' part is secondary to the 'hooligan' part. Don't get me wrong, I'm a City fan through and through but when it comes to making the choice between my club or my firm then I'll choose the Guvnors any day of the week. Saying that though, I think we won 3–1 so maybe I should have gone.

While the team were busy scoring goals on our behalf, we were struggling to get the upper hand against Grimsby's firm. They were putting up more of a fight than we had bargained for and the action eventually spilled out into the maze of alleyways and back streets surrounding their ground. The local police weren't used to dealing with football violence on that scale and it took them the full ninety minutes to get it under control. There were a couple of Old Bill here and there during the game but they didn't want to get their hands dirty.

Shortly after the match finished, the Five-O swamped the streets and forced us into an escort. Grimsby had done pretty fucking well. They'd managed to draw with us, quite a feat for a little team. We had grossly underestimated our opponents and it had cost us our victory.

Once we got to the station, we managed to break free from the escort and we tried to organise another bout of violence with Grimsby but they weren't having it.

'We'll meet you over in Cleethorpes. There'll be a lot less Old Bill round those sides,' I told them.

'It's not Grimsby,' they protested. It was as if the rest of the world was an unknown quantity and they were scared to leave their own back-yard. Cleethorpes is only a couple of miles away. I couldn't see what the problem was. They should have overridden their fear of leaving their shitty little third-rate Blackpool and had a second round but, then again, if they want to spend the rest of their lives confined to a place where electricity is regarded as a novelty then that's up to them.

Despite their unwillingness to leave their comfort zone, Grimsby's firm were actually a damn sight better than we had given them credit for. I've always had a strong affinity for the underdog and that's what Grimsby were. They were from a place that conjures up images of depressing, litter-strewn beaches and people with sisters who are also their mothers but they could hold their own in a fight. So 'Jack', if you're reading this, your introduction was fucking weird and your firm needs to stop turning out in stupid colours but, apart from that, you've got yourself a decent set of lads.

Grimsby the place is a shit hole but Grimsby the firm are definitely one to watch.

22

LISA

One of the reasons the Guvnors have played such an important role in my life is that they've always been there for me when things have taken a turn for the worse. A lot of people think their friends have got their backs, but how do they know for sure when they've never been in a life-or-death situation? My fellow hooligans were the family I never had and their loyalty was put to the test over and over again. That said, there's a big difference between the love you get from your mates and the love that can come only from a woman. I've never been into all that lovey-dovey nonsense but there was one girl who made me feel like I was onto a winner.

Her name was Lisa. She was my first love.

A lot of so-called 'hard men' like to think of themselves as completely and utterly lacking in any form of emotion. They try to act like cold, heartless individuals, who would laugh at the idea of showing affection but they aren't fooling anybody. We are all created with an inbuilt desire to be loved and hooligans are no different. The first time I laid eyes on Lisa, back in 1988, I thought, 'She's a bit of all right.' I didn't for a single minute expect that she would end up being the mother of my child. When you're a bloke, you think with your genitals first and your brain much later. My initial reaction was to strike up a conversation in the hope that I could slick talk my way into her knickers.

'Have you got a spare cig?' I asked, half expecting her to say no. She was standing in Piccadilly Gardens and I was wandering the streets during a period of homelessness. I scarcely had a penny to my name and I really did need a fag. It wasn't just a random icebreaker.

'Yeah, sure. You're called Benny aren't you?'

Eh? How did she know my name? I was praying she hadn't seen me in the papers for weighing somebody in at the football.

'Oh I live in Wythenshawe,' she explained, sensing that I was wracking my brains, trying to figure out where she might have known me from. 'I know a couple of people that you know.'

I was living in Manchester airport at the time, which is on the edge of Wythenshawe. It was nice and warm and they had a comfortable set of benches that were perfect for me to sleep on. I was homeless again by choice. I had moved out of my flat in Whalley Range because it was proper bare, with no cooker or anything. I'd been kipping at Frankie's house, which was all well and good until I began to feel like I was taking liberties. I decided I would have to find another place of my own. The airport wasn't exactly a luxury apartment but it was better than sleeping rough. Nobody ever mithered me and I never had any trouble there. I sprawled out on the benches every night and pretended I had fallen asleep waiting for a flight.

The next time I saw Lisa, she was at a Happy Mondays concert and because I was selling tickets she must have thought I had something to do with the band.

'Do you work in the music industry then?' she asked. She was a very musical person.[29] She was into the whole 'Madchester' movement and was a regular at the Hacienda and a couple of the other legendary early Nineties venues.

'Erm yeah,' I told her, 'Something like that.'[30]

She looked impressed.

'So who's the next big band to come out of Manchester then?'

Fuck! It was time for an educated guess.

'Erm, the Stone Roses?' I told her. I was spot on as well. A couple of months down the line, they were doing gigs up and down the country

---

[29] She's in a band called Esoteric Gender nowadays, who are doing pretty well for themselves. Check them out at http://www.theesotericgender.com. I recommend them.

[30] Don't try and tell me that you've never lied to try and impress a girl. We've all done it at some point in our lives.

and they were on the radio every other song. She must have thought I was clued up.

Lisa frequented the same types of places as me and I kept bumping into her when I was working the in-out. Every time I saw her, we talked about the music scene and I'd feed her little titbits of phoney information about the artists. She was a pretty girl and I would have been a fool not to make a move but I didn't even have a house to take her back to. I had recently moved into a hostel in Wythenshawe as I'd grown weary of living in the airport and on mates' floors. I was still waiting on a council flat and I was effectively homeless. Then there was the whole football thing. There aren't a lot of women who will put up with a bloke who goes out fighting every weekend. But then again, if she knew my friends from Wythenshawe she surely must have known what type of life I led.

As it turned out, Lisa knew exactly what I got up to on a Saturday and she was perfectly relaxed about it.

'Well you're a thug but you're funny and intelligent as well,' she told me.

A lot of girls would feel as if they were in direct competition with the Guvnors but she didn't seem bothered that I had such an all-encompassing pastime. So long as I never expressed my violent side around her, she couldn't care less that I liked to beat people up for fun. Everybody has their quirks and she accepted hooliganism as one of mine.

By the time we started going out, me and Lisa knew each other inside out. She was difficult to shock, which meant that I could tell her all the gritty details. She never put any pressure on me to act in a certain way. She liked me exactly how I was. It would have been a romance made in heaven if it wasn't for the fact I was living in a hostel and she lived with her strict Catholic grandma, who didn't her like having me round at her place. I usually ended up climbing through the window to see her, which made our relationship a bit like Romeo and Juliet. I suppose it was a sign of how much we wanted to be with one another. If a girl's worth going out with she's worth sneaking around in the dark for.

I was living in a hostel during the initial stages of our relationship but that didn't mean my pockets were always empty. I was managing to hustle up a regular wage from selling tickets and swag outside the concerts, which meant that I was able to take Lisa to the Palace theatre any time there was a decent play on. We were always going to the Hacienda as well. Music was her passion. She was a talented singer and loved to watch the local bands. It's funny because if it wasn't for a member of what has now become the most successful band ever to come out of Manchester, I wouldn't have been able to spend half as much time with her. One of my close acquaintances at the time was the lead singer for a little known indie outfit called Oasis. He'd knocked about in Gorton as a kid and he was a football lad way before he was a celebrity. Noel Gallagher was one of the original Young Guvnors, before we even had a name for ourselves, and, as it happened, he had just moved into a brand new block of flats on Whitworth Street in Manchester city centre.

'Why don't you put your name down on the waiting list?' Noel asked me. 'India House the flats are called. They're proper posh yuppie flats, seriously. You want to get yourself one before the word spreads.'

Looking back, it's funny to think that a man who is now earning millions used to consider a city-centre council flat the height of sophis-tication. Saying that though, they were a step above your average council house. I followed his advice and put my name down for an apartment. Before I knew it, I'd gone from living in a hostel to living in a plush flat in the middle of Manchester.

Now that I had a place of my own, everything about my relation-ship with Lisa was perfect. Or at least it should have been. We could see each other as often as we wanted to and we didn't need to sneak around like naughty teenagers. But something felt wrong. Lisa was the first person who had ever truly loved me and I couldn't handle it. My self-esteem had been eroded to the point where I couldn't get my head around the fact that somebody could love me as much as she did. I wasn't sure if I liked the idea of being in love. It was unfamiliar territory. I was genuinely scared.

When you've spent the formative years of your life being told that you're a failure, it makes it difficult to accept that there are people who will accept you for who you are. Lisa knew I was a thug and she knew I was a crook. I'd even taken her abroad on shoplifting expeditions to

Germany and Belgium. She didn't steal anything but she didn't have any objections to me earning a living through crime. There was nothing I could tell her about my life that would have fazed her. She didn't care how I made my money, as long as I treated her with respect. Saying that though, there's only so much that any one person can take, regardless of how accepting they are of other people's flaws. I was living in a world of violence, excess and extreme hedonism. And it was about to come tumbling down.

There will come a time in every hooligan's life when the Old Bill gets the better of him. He will end up getting jailed or banned or, in my case, both. The police have got the biggest firm in England and they don't give a fuck about taking liberties. If a copper hits you he is upholding the law but if you hit a copper then all hell breaks loose and it's plastered across the front pages. Even the sturdiest of relationships can only take so much. Jail is one thing but being banned from the one activity that makes you feel alive is enough to wipe any notion of a happy life off the slate. Lisa didn't care about me getting locked up, but it was how I reacted to being banned from football that drove her away.

It all started after a run-in with the Red Army.

23

THE PICCADILLY INCIDENT

It was a typical Saturday night in 1988. City and United were out on the town. Pissed-up hooligans staggered around among your usual mix of drunken revellers and then, inevitably, the two firms met. There was only one possible outcome: utter carnage. Fists and bottles flew, the streets descended into bedlam.

'Come on then you blue bastards,' yelled a knife-wielding United lad. He arched his sharp blade through the cold, night air and sliced two of our older lads apart.

'Argh my fucking kidneys,' yelped a heavily bleeding Guvnor, clutching at his side as he hobbled down the street to safety.

I wasn't there but I was told the Munichs surrounded their victims before striking, taking advantage of the fact that the lads that they attacked had got separated from the rest of the group during the commotion. They could have weighed them in without the need for weapons. It was one of the worst liberties anyone ever took with the Guvnors. We were going to have to teach those sneaky Red cunts a lesson that they would never forget. There is a rigid set of rules associated with membership of a football firm and they had flouted them.

The following Saturday, United were playing against Arsenal at Highbury. It was the perfect opportunity to bushwhack them. We were at home to Plymouth so we would have a mob in town when they got back to Manchester. We hatched a plan to attack them at Piccadilly. This time we would be tooled up to fuck and there would be no holding back. They weren't the only ones that could go around slashing people. Two could play that game.

The Munichs' blatant liberty-taking had angered us no end. The lads who had got slashed could look after themselves, and they didn't think much of it, but that was hardly the point. Their attackers had transgressed against the code and had to be held accountable.

I was proper looking forward to settling the score and as their train pulled up into Piccadilly sixty shadowy figures lurked in the dark, plotting their demise. United jumped off and headed for the exit, hanging around at the doors until the mob was back together. The minute they reached London Road, there was an almighty cry of 'Guvnors' and we came running towards them, whacking them with sticks and sending them scurrying back inside the station.

The so-called Red Army carried on running all the way through the ticket barriers and onto the platforms, with an angry mob of Guvnors hot on their heels. During the pursuit, one of the Munichs tripped and a couple of our older faces grabbed him, ready to do him. Fortunately for their captive, he was a lad I knew from Gorton. I wasn't prepared to let them weigh him in.

'Let him go. We have liberties taken on us. We don't take liberties with other people.'

The older lads walked off in a huff, disappointed they hadn't got to batter him.

'Listen, go home,' I told the terrified Munich. 'And don't come back because we're out for revenge tonight and we've got a good mob with us.'

By this stage, the coppers had the situation under control and United had forged a hasty retreat. What a bunch of cowards. They had denied us our night of vengeance and we were still proper up for it with nobody left to fight.

'Come on, fight me,' a voice behind us said.

This sounded promising. I was itching for a row and didn't give a fuck who I took on.

The problem was that the voice belonged to a copper. He was standing in a big group of dibble a few feet away. It was hardly an invitation I was able to take up. What if I came out on top? I'd get sent down for assaulting a police officer. It was a no-win situation.

'You think you're hard in a gang,' the copper sneered. He was one to talk. There were a lot of his colleagues close by and he could call for back-up on his radio at any time.

'You're all fucking soft,' he taunted.

What the fuck was this cunt on?

He obviously thought he could wind us up without any comeback, and he could have done just that, but he wasn't content with verbals. The daft twat poked his truncheon hard into the small of Clanger's back. It's one thing giving someone an earful of abuse. You can ignore somebody telling you that you're soft, but it's a different story when they're bashing you in the spine with a baton. He had deliberately instigated a fight, not what you'd expect from someone paid to enforce the law.

Clanger spun around, pulled a hammer out of his pocket and smashed the nearest Old Bill across the head. I don't even know if it was the copper who had poked him, but he took the brunt of it anyway. Because you wear a uniform it doesn't mean you can deliberately pro-voke people into kicking off with you in the hope that you can arrest them for it. If you go around poking groups of football hooligans with a big fuck-off stick you can hardly complain when you, or one of your mates, get a sore head. I'm not condoning what Clanger did but it was the fault of the Old Bill. They should have left us well alone.

The dibble's face froze in a picture of shock and horror as the hammer made contact. His eyes slowly closed and he slumped to the ground, unconscious. As soon as he he hit the floor, his colleagues tried to nab us. I wasn't going to let these navy-blue Hitlers arrest us for defending ourselves and, when they came within arm's length, I cracked one of them around the head with a Lucozade bottle and punched him and kicked him for all I was worth while he was on his way to the ground. This was in the days when Lucozade still came in the original glass containers. They were hard as a rock and capable of doing some serious damage. I kept a tight grip on the bottle after I'd hit him with it, secretly hoping that the glass had cracked so that I could ram the jagged edge into his face. Unfortunately, I was denied that pleasure.

At the time, I was reacting on instinct and couldn't have given a fuck about the dibble's wellbeing. With the benefit of hindsight, I now think that he and the rest of the coppers got a raw deal, as it was their big-mouth pal who was at fault. They were only coming to the aid of a fallen comrade.

Moments later, the piercing scream of police sirens filled the air and a riot van skidded to a halt outside Piccadilly. It was time for us to make a swift departure. We quickly slunk out of the station and headed over to the Cyprus Tavern to see if there were any United there.

The Cyprus was empty, which was a major disappointment. We were fired up after our run-in with the coppers and twatting a couple of Munichs would have been the icing on the cake.

'Let's go home,' I suggested to the lads.

We had been deprived of yet another opportunity for revenge. United are always going on about how they're the superior firm and making out we've never brought it to them. Well they must have known that we'd be heading to the Cyprus. We weren't exactly going to leave the city centre as soon as the coppers had got there so if they're such a super firm why didn't they stand and face us? They're always willing to have it when they've got a couple of hundred Cockneys to back them up so why couldn't they stand their ground when it was Mancs versus Mancs?

The following morning, I woke up feeling angry that we hadn't got to teach the Munichs a lesson. We'd chased them off the streets and into the station but we'd missed out on the chance to properly go to work on them. Oh well. Maybe a spot of early-morning telly would cheer me up. Or maybe not, as the incident with the hammer was the main story on the local news.

'Violent football thugs assault a defenceless police officer,' the newsreader announced.

Eh? It was a dibble who had started it.

'The policeman is suffering from a fractured skull and broken ribs. The culprits are thought to be well-known football hooligans,' the report went on.

A clip of the cop with his head in a massive, over-the-top bandage flashed up on the screen.

'A hero policeman took on a mob of *sixty* soccer thugs single-handed to protect fellow officers,' wrote that temple of journalistic integrity,

The Sun. 'The . . . British Transport policeman . . . needed an emergency operation to remove a bone that was pressing on his brain.'

The cop was treated like an injured war hero. There were pictures of him in the local papers with his family stood around his hospital bed. If you ask me, there should have been an investigation into the motives behind the attack. One of the cops in Piccadilly that day took it upon himself to provoke us and to assault us, which resulted in his colleague being taken to hospital. Am I glad he got injured? The answer is no. He no doubt had a family and they shouldn't have had to see him like that. Could it have been prevented? Fucking right it could. The cop responsible for assaulting Clanger could have let us walk away from the station without trying to bully us.

From that day on, the coppers were out to get us. They knew who had been involved in the assault on their colleague and they were determined to punish us. When rival football hooligans are out to get you, you can arm yourself with CS gas, ready to defend yourself. When the Old Bill are gunning for you, there's nothing that you can do. If you retaliate, they will radio for back up and, as I've said before, they've got the biggest firm in the country. The Five-O were intent on dishing out their own brand of rough justice. I was powerless to stop them.

A couple of weeks later, a pair of dibble spotted me on the approach to the station and immediately started issuing threats.

'You're only hard when you're with your mates,' dibble number one sneered, obviously having learnt nothing from what had happened at Piccadilly.

'Yeah, if you're that hard, come around the corner for a one on one,' spouted dibble number two, who appeared to be attempting to impress the other officer.

'I'll gladly fight you both,' I told them, 'but what if I win? What will happen then? You'll fucking nick me, that's what. What would I have to gain by having a straightener with you? Even if I win, I lose.'

The coppers weren't listening.

'Come on, fight me,' screamed dibble number one.

There was only one thing for it. I was going to have to find a witness so that they couldn't drag me around the corner and weigh me in.

'Eeyah, watch this,' I shouted to a passer-by, drawing her attention to the harassment. 'These coppers are going to batter me. Keep your eyes on them. They're just about to do it.'

The two Old Bill looked proper flustered.

'Walk away,' they told me. 'Just walk away now.'

They were obviously worried that the general public were going to get to see their true colours. I did as they said and carried on walking. God knows what they would have done if that woman hadn't been passing.

I may have got the better of the cops on that occasion but they were about to deliver me a fatal blow. Being attacked is one thing but having your freedom taken away is an entirely different matter. The coppers might not have been able to do me over but they had the law on their side and they were determined to destroy me. Punch me in my face and you will break my skin. Ban me from the matches and lock me in a cell and you will take away my soul.

And that's exactly what they did.

24

OPERATION OMEGA

'Omega' is the final letter of the Greek alphabet. It was also the final straw for us, as it was the name that Greater Manchester Police gave to the undercover operation aimed at taking the Guvnors off the streets. Eighty of our lads were charged with a variety of offences, ranging from 'gaining pecuniary advantage' (jibbing the trains) to attempted murder. Because it was the first operation of its kind, the coppers knew they needed to make it work to secure funding for similar initiatives in the years to come. We were their guinea pigs and the longer they could lock us away for, the more successful they would be deemed to be.

The Guvnors were a thorn in the side of the authorities. Pubs were getting trashed, stations were being overrun and Old Bill were being smashed around the head with hammers and Lucozade bottles. The first step towards putting us behind bars was for them to correctly identify us. The British Transport Police knew us all by name and they would have been the perfect candidates to head the operation but the Greater Manchester Police wanted the credit and so they wasted a lot of time by re-gathering the information the BTP already had. They had two hundred and fifty of us nicked at West Ham for a made-up reason, got our names and addresses, took our pictures and then released us without charge. I remember thinking at the time that it was a strange thing to do. If they've gone to the trouble of making an arrest, the coppers will usually have you for something. It was the first phase of Omega, the beginning of the end.

The Manchester Old Bill would like you to believe they infiltrated our mob with undercover officers. Did they fuck. They stood out like a sore thumb and the only members of the firm who believed that they were hooligans were a couple of random pissheads on the fringes. There was one geezer they kept buying drinks for in the hope that he would tell them where we were meeting. He wasn't even a proper Young Guvnor; he was a random alky with a penchant for telling lies.

'I'm well in with the Guvnors,' he told them, 'One of the main lads is my best mate. You should come to a match with us. We'll show you how it's done.'

The first time I was aware that the Old Bill were in tow was during a game against Aston Villa in August 1987 when two dodgy characters struck up a conversation with us out of the blue.

'Benny and Spinner here today, are they?' one of them asked.

What a bizarre question for a total stranger to come out with. He would have known who I was if he was anything to do with the Guvnors.

'Who the fuck are you?' I replied.

He wasn't one of us. I'd never seen him before in my life.

'Right, get these two separated,' I instructed the other members of the firm. 'It's time to find out who they are and what they're doing here.'

We started off by asking the two Old Bill how they knew each other. It was a simple question but they were stumped. So much for them being the masters of undercover operations.

'You best fuck off. There's something not quite right about you two. I'll be keeping a keen eye on the both of you,' I warned them.

The two undercovers carried on turning up at matches until we eventually had to threaten them to get them to leave us alone. A lad called Shady Ady put a comb to one of their bellies and told him he was going to slice his stomach open if he ever saw him again. When you've got a metal object pressed against your gut, you rarely have the time to consider whether it's the genuine article. You just assume that it's a blade.

'If I ever see you trying to get on the train to a game with us again, I'll stab you up and throw you out of the door,' Ady told the copper and that was the last that we ever saw of the cunt. That dibble ended up on Prozac and he is currently seeing a doctor for post-traumatic stress disorder. That'll teach him to be so inexcusably shit at his job![31]

When the Old Bill finally raided our houses, we were half expecting it. It was six in the morning and they booted my door clean off. It was over the top. They had two riot vans and there were police dogs all over the place. They were treating me like a mafia boss, although for some weird reason I wasn't that stressed. In fact I was mildly annoyed because the coppers wouldn't give me a light for my cig.

They picked up four hundred-odd people[32], although only eighty of us were ever charged. Talk about fucking overkill. They were seizing people's belongings right, left and centre as well. One of the lads had a brick in a bag taken from his house under the bizarre logic that it could have been used as a weapon. They had very little evidence. They were clutching at straws.

'A frightening array of weapons including flick knives, hammers, coshes and body armour has been recovered,' wrote the *Manchester Evening News*. What the reporter neglected to mention was that the lad who had the body armour was a Thai boxer and he needed it for training.

'One of those detained is a man wanted in connection with an incident at the City–Crystal Palace game at Maine Road last December 5 when a match official was seriously injured,' the paper went on. 'He is thought to have been hit by a coin.' Well what a serious injury that is. He was lucky to survive!

While the press were busy picking us apart, the coppers were desperately trying to scare us into bubbling.

---

[31] Several of the coppers who worked on Omega ended up suffering from mental illnesses. 'An undercover detective who infiltrated a gang of soccer hooligans suffered a breakdown because of the fear of being exposed,' journalist Paul Horrocks wrote in the *Manchester Evening News*. 'He spent several weeks posing as a soccer thug attached to Manchester City louts known as the Guvnors and the Young Guvnors.' They were making him sound like Donnie Brasco. 'Mr David Sumner, prosecuting, said that, in August 1987, undercover officers infiltrated and monitored the activities of the gangs. They showed a "remarkable degree of courage" and witnessed appalling violence, but were unable to intervene.'

[32] Not all of these people were actually arrested; some of them were merely questioned about certain incidents.

'It's funny that you're going to all of these faraway places and yet you seem to be bumping into the same set of people whatever city you're in,' one of the Old Bill suggested to me, as if that proved I was a thug.

'Well I support Man City and they're all City fans. We all go in the same end so we're bound to see each other at most of the matches,' I replied.

What a fucking numpty. If you're mates with somebody then you're going to be seen in the same place. It doesn't mean you're committing a crime together. You might just enjoy each other's company.

I was remanded for just over a week before being granted bail.

'You're free to go,' announced the judge, although the dibble had other ideas. 'Hold on a minute Mr Bennion,' one of their officers instructed as I was leaving the courtroom. 'We need to question you regarding a rather serious incident at Piccadilly station in which a number of our officers were assaulted.'

The Old Bill shoved me into the back of a police car and drove me to Piccadilly, where the BTP bought me a McDonald's for my tea and interviewed me about the attack. They initially tried to charge me with attempted murder but they soon dropped the charge to conspiring to commit violent disorder. I was given bail for the Piccadilly incident as well as the violent disorder that I had supposedly been involved in while the undercover Old Bill had been with us. I was also hit with an eight-till-eight curfew and banned from every football ground and licensed premises in the country until the trial started.

One of the bail conditions was that I had to sign in every Saturday at the local police station. Two words: fuck that. I wanted to go to our away game at Brighton so I attempted to get a doctor's note, which would give me an excuse for not turning up at the cop shop.

'I can hardly write a letter saying that you're poorly when there's no physical signs of you being unwell,' the doctor told me. 'I can write a letter saying you've been to see me and that you claim to be under the weather. That's the best I can do for you.'

It would have to do. I had no other option.

'Go on then,' I sighed, attempting to look as ill as possible. 'That's good enough for me.'

When I got the note home and read it, I noticed that it wasn't dated. It was as good as useless and I didn't even bother handing it in at the station. I figured that I'd be better off going to the game without letting on to the coppers because that way there was a slim chance that I'd be able to pass below the radar.

I was half expecting the Old Bill to be waiting outside my house the minute I got back from Brighton, but they weren't. I spent the next few days bracing myself for my door being kicked in but there was still no sign of them. That's when it hit me. They didn't know when my court date was. They probably thought the case had already been tried and assumed I'd stopped signing in because I'd been locked up. That was the last time I considered signing in, although I eventually went along and told them that I wasn't going to comply with the bail conditions. I couldn't be arsed waiting around for the outcome of the hearing. I was sick of worrying about doing time. I felt that I might as well get a couple of months of jail time under my belt before the verdict was delivered. They remanded me in Strangeways. I stayed there until my sentencing date.

The whole judicial process was a farce. We were originally supposed to be tried at Manchester Crown Court but the authorities suddenly decided that the dock wasn't big enough to hold the twenty-six Young Guvnors that were due in court that day and we were told it was being moved to Preston Crown Court. Fair enough, I thought. One court is as good as another. Then they changed it to Lancaster. What were these cunts playing at? That was when they dropped the final bombshell. 'They're saying that Lancaster isn't big enough either. They're on about having the trial in Liverpool,' my solicitor informed me.

A couple of months earlier, English football had suffered a major trauma: the Hillsborough-stadium disaster. Before the official report into that tragedy was published, hooligans were getting the blame for what happened that terrible day in Sheffield.[33] Quite clearly, the

---

33 The Hillsborough disaster took place on 15 April 1989 in Sheffield. Ninety-six Liverpool fans were crushed to death before the FA Cup semi-final with Nottingham Forest. The *Taylor Report* into the causes of the tragedy found that fans had not been to blame. Rather Lord Taylor was heavily critical of the game's policing.

coppers were trying to stitch us up. They were hoping that the Scousers would think that people like us were responsible for what had happened at Hillsborough and that they'd find us guilty of the Omega charges no matter what.

Luckily the Mickeys are smarter than they look. They knew full well that Hillsborough had taken place because of poor planning on the part of the authorities and they refused to be taken in by the tabloids' feeble attempts to point the finger at us. Still, sending a group of Mancs to a courthouse in Liverpool pretty much eliminates any chance of them getting a fair trial. The Old Bill were out to get us and they were willing to use every dirty trick in the book.

Because there were so many of us in the dock, the judge decided that we would have to make do with four solicitors between us, which was another fucking piss take. We weren't even being charged with the same set of offences. It was their way of depriving us of proper legal representation.

The straw that broke the camel's back came when the judge gave a long lecture about our attitude to the press.

'It has come to my attention that a serious incident has happened outside this very building. I have received information that one of the defendants has threatened to take a knife to a reporter and quite frankly, this disgusts me. I will have no bullyboy tactics within my courtroom. This court is for freedom and the light of democracy will always continue to shine.'

What about the dibble then? They were allowed to give their statements from behind a protective screen to preserve their anonymity. The papers weren't allowed to print their pictures so why were they allowed to publish ours? We were yet to be convicted of any act of wrongdoing and, for all they knew, we had been wrongly accused. Why were they allowed to publicly brand us as hooligans when we hadn't received our guilty verdicts yet? The 'light of democracy' my fucking arse. It was one rule for them and another rule for us.

The evidence that the coppers produced during the trial was fucking dire.

'We were unable to take detailed notes at the scene of the disturbances. It would have drawn attention to us and blown our cover.'

We knew who they were anyway. They weren't exactly masters of disguise.

'We had to scribble a vague outline of the day's events down on beer mats and type them up later that day. Difficult policing conditions called for rather unorthodox methods of recording our evidence.'

So a couple of doodles on a beer mat counts as evidence does it? What a fucking joke.

On 5 June 1989 we were all found guilty, despite the fact there was no real proof against us. There was proof that we were dedicated football fans and that we were always at games together but that was the only thing they had on us. What really made my blood boil was that United were arrested during similar raids a couple of months down the line and the judge who presided over their trial ruled that it was unlawful for the Old Bill to remain anonymous. The case against them was eventually dropped and they all walked free.

Several members of the firm were also convicted of offences related to the Piccadilly incident, although the prosecution commented that it was 'quite clear that the ringleaders were not in the dock'. His assessment would have probably gone in our favour if he hadn't then gone on to peddle a load of bollocks about how we'd supposedly tried to 'lure' the copper away from the station so that we could do him in.

'There is no need to tell you what the public at large think of thugs,' the judge told Clanger. 'You have committed a wicked and cowardly offence.'

Well if losing your rag when some knobhead in a uniform is trying to wind you up is 'wicked and cowardly' then I'm as much of a wicked coward as the next man.

The local papers heralded our guilty verdicts as a major step towards eliminating football violence. 'One-hundred-year ban for hooligan gang,' the tabloids proudly proclaimed, although I know for a fact that the police would have rather the headlines read, 'One hundred years in jail each.' The highest ban that anybody got was fifteen years. There were a couple of tens but most of the firm got sevens.

With the issue of bans from football covered, the court moved on to dish out prison sentences. Clanger ended up getting three years for the hammer attack, which was good because he was expecting to get ten.

I got a six-month suspended sentence for the disturbances at the games and ten months for the Piccadilly incident. The only saving grace was that I'd spent so many months on remand that the jail time was out of the way by the time the verdicts were announced. When the judge read our sentences out I was proper buzzing. It was June and there was no football on, so the banning order was the last thing on my mind. I also had a £300 fine to pay but that was fuck all in the scheme of things.

I was free at last, although the worst was yet to come.

25

LIFE AFTER FOOTBALL

We were in high spirits when we walked out of the courtroom for the last time. A huge entourage of City fans had gathered to watch our trial and we immediately headed to the pub to celebrate our release. Impossible bail conditions, dodgy evidence, sitting around bored in a six-foot-by-eight-foot cell all day. The coppers had left their mark but it was over now and we were able to put the whole ordeal behind us.

Or so we thought.

At this point, I hadn't even stopped to consider the fact that I was banned from the one thing that made my life worthwhile. It hadn't sunk in and for once things were going surprisingly well. Me and Lisa were still very much in love, I had a roof over my head and I had just arranged to go abroad on a shoplifting trip with Frankie. Everything was as it should have been.

Ducking and diving was the only realistic way of earning a living now that I was unable to tout for tickets outside the matches. They didn't have closed-circuit-television cameras in those days and the Continental clothes stores were easy to steal from. We'd go into a shop with a pair of wire snips concealed in a rucksack, take ten pairs of jeans into the changing rooms with us, cut the tags off, shove the jeans inside the bag and fuck off back to our hotel room. They were putting pairs of trainers out on display in places like Germany and Belgium as well, which meant that we were also able to go out robbing footwear. Getting there was cheap and there were a couple of ways to travel. You could get a train to Dover and pay £24 for the ferry to France or there was a budget airline that had tickets to Germany for £69. Once I got back home, I'd either go round the pubs selling what I'd stolen or ask my mates if they wanted cheap clothes, which guaranteed me a hefty profit out of every robbing spree.

Our journeys abroad were a business trip and holiday rolled into one, although I was now going to have to start grafting twice as hard. Lisa had some momentous news.

'I'm pregnant,' she told me.

The moment the words left her mouth, I knew my life would never be the same again. I took a couple of minutes to absorb the enormity of what I had been told. I was about to have a son.

Stephen was born in 1990, roughly a year after I came out of jail. He was blue when he first came out and he was choking, which gave me a scare, but then he managed to catch his breath and he was okay after that. He had a fine head of blond hair and he smiled as soon as he saw me. The nurse tried to tell me that he was pulling a funny face because he needed burping, but it was definitely a smile!

Words can't begin to describe a father's love for his child and from the first time I laid eyes on him, I was determined to give him the childhood I never had.

'Look son, that's Maine Road,' I told him, lifting him up so that he could see the stadium from the hospital window. 'One day I'm going to take you there to see your first football match.'

Stephen and I were inseparable. Some people will go to the pub and say, 'I've managed to get away from the missus and the baby for a while,' but I would have spent every waking minute with him if I hadn't had to go out grafting. It was amazing to think I'd brought a little person into the world, although it brought a lot of painful memories along with it. Why had my mother never loved me the way that I loved Stephen? My childhood and Stephen's childhood couldn't have been more different. By the age of four, I had run away from home at least six times. I never got to experience a mother's love and it hurt me.

Lisa was studying, as well as working three nights a week as a barmaid, so I was left to look after Stephen most of the time. I bought him Lego and a brand new Scalextric and we would while away the hours playing with his toys. Every minute I spent with him was special because I was giving him something I'd never had. Unfortunately, I was also spending more and more time with something I loved almost as much as I loved my family and it was about to deprive me of my girlfriend, my son, my health and my money. When you're used to the rush that comes from football violence, it's impossible to carry on living as if you've never experienced it. You have to get your kicks from somewhere and drugs were as good an alternative as any. Before I knew it, I was a fully-fledged amphetamine addict and I was taking four ounces of whiz a week, at a cost of £160 an ounce.

Up to that point, I had only ever taken drugs on a recreational basis. I'd experimented with everything from cannabis to heroin but nothing I tried ever came close to that rush of adrenaline you get when you're standing shoulder to shoulder with your mates, waiting for it to go off. Now that going to the football was off limits, the only way that I could add a little excitement to my life was by getting off my face on whiz. I hammered it day and night.

Before I knew it, I was a raging phet-head.

My childhood experiences made me particularly prone to drug addiction. I was used to coping with a high degree of stress and the buzz I got from amphetamines made me alert, like when I was afraid. I'm not trying to justify my decision to devote my life to drugs. I'm attempting to explain why I am the way I am. People probably think, 'How can you get yourself addicted to a class-B drug like speed?' Well let me tell you this. If the government knew how persuasive a substance it is amphetamine would be ranked alongside crack and heroin. First there is the little high that lifts you into the clouds. You feel as if you could gently drift along forever and then you reach a certain brain frequency that makes you feel like you're 'on one', in the words of Big Audio Dynamite.[34]

I did a variety of things to support my habit. I worked the in-out at pop concerts, which earned me around £600 a day, and there was always some kind of event on somewhere in the north-west, whether it was a major international act playing at a high-capacity stadium or a bunch of Z-list celebrities performing at Warrington town hall. I must have made more money selling merchandise outside the gigs than the

---

[34] An Eighties post-punk group formed by Mick Jones of The Clash.

bands did. I remember when INXS were playing in Manchester and I'd bought a load of T-shirts to sell. The problem was that I couldn't get near the venue to flog them because of the security guards. I was just about to give up and head home when I noticed coach loads of fans stuck in a traffic jam at the other end of the road. Bingo! They were far enough away from the concert for me to peddle my wares. I made £100 from the first coach in the space of about five minutes and then I went to the coach behind it and made myself another ton.

When I wasn't selling swag, I was buying and selling things from auction houses. I've always had an entrepreneurial streak, a little like Arfur Daley from *Minder*. I wasn't one of those addicts who would go around mugging old ladies and making a nuisance of themselves. Most of the grafting I did was harmless. Sure I stole a few pairs of trainers from the shops and I sold a couple of hooky tracksuits. But I never did anything majorly illegal. I stayed within the boundaries of my conscience and the only people that I hurt were myself and Lisa.

After a while, I started knocking out a couple of bags of whiz to my mates, just to make an extra bit of change. At first it was only little bits and bobs but because people knew that I was on drugs, they were always asking me if I could get them this, that or the other. As the months went by, more and more users started coming to me for phet, until I was doubling my money on every gram I sold. In fact I earned as much as I was getting off the dole in a single morning. I was still living in my plush city-centre flat and didn't want anybody coming round to my house so I'd always meet my clients either on the street or round at their gaffs.

I wasn't the type of dealer who would break people's legs if they were a few hours late with a payment. I made a point of telling my customers that I was selling on behalf of somebody further up the ladder. That way I could tell them that my boss was looking to have a 'word' if they ever started fucking me about. Everybody knew I could be a bit of a nutter and they must have reasoned that if Benny is working for someone else then that someone must be a *real* nutter. Whenever anybody tried to have me off, I'd ring up and scare the shit out of them.

'He's probably been around already, hasn't he? I told him not to hurt your dad but he wouldn't listen. He's not done what he said he was going to do to him, has he?'

It was a sure-fire way to collect what I was owed.

Because I was inventive with my scare tactics, I never had to resort to violence. People have a preconceived image of a drug dealer as somebody who goes around bullying clients into parting with cash but it's not like that and, besides, I wasn't a fully fledged dealer. I was selling to make enough to support my habit and that was it.

The more drugs I sold, the more money I spent on them until it got to the stage where I was attempting to maximise my high by injecting speed directly into my veins. I'd seen a couple of my mates whacking it up and they told me how much more of a buzz you got. They weren't wrong either. The moment you've injected yourself with whiz, you can never go back to taking it orally. The buzz is instantaneous. There's nothing like it. You feel completely energised from head to toe and suddenly the only thing that matters in your life is drugs. Any notion that you will ever stop taking amphetamines goes immediately out of the window.

One of the many downsides to whacking a needle into your arm is that you end up with bruises on your skin from where you've missed the veins. Within a matter of months, I was stick thin, constantly sweating and covered from head to toe in track marks. It was time to swallow my pride and book an appointment with my doctor. I didn't like the direction my life was taking. I needed professional help.

'I'm putting you on a prescription of Dexedrine pills,' my doctor told me. 'They're a controlled form of amphetamine and they're a lot less harmful than street drugs.'

The tablets were designed to provide me with just enough of a buzz to get me through the day. The problem was that I was used to being permanently wired. Like fuck I was going to stop taking the phet. Fair enough, the Dexedrine pills were a landmark in that they marked my first genuine attempt to stop taking speed but they were unlikely to help me to overcome my addiction. For me, they were a cheaper way of getting high.

My habit grew to the point where it began to affect the relationship with my family. I sold our £350 television set. I started smelling badly because I was sweating so much. I became an unpleasant person to be around. At first I thought that Lisa didn't mind me being an addict. When you're off your head on drugs all the time, you become oblivious to the people around you. I was arrogant enough to believe that she would love me no matter what I did but boy was I mistaken. The first time I realised our relationship was on the rocks was when she got her sister's boyfriend to change the lock on our door while I was out collecting my Dexedrine prescription. It was her less-than-subtle way of hammering home the message that it was over.

I was furious that Lisa had tried to lock me out of my own flat and so I immediately set about smashing my way in to let her know how angry I was. Just as I'd finished kicking and punching my way through the door, her sister's boyfriend turned up with the Five-O in tow and the Old Bill dragged me outside.

'I'm going to get you for this,' I shouted. 'I'm going to fucking have you, you dirty grassing bastard.'

When the coppers had finally let me out of the cells again, I con- sidered going round to the grass's house and smashing his television with a baseball bat. However, one of my straight-goer friends talked me out of it. In hindsight, I should have gone round there because it later transpired that he had told the coppers that I'd threatened to have him shot. His statement was produced in a subsequent court case as proof of my bad character and it didn't exactly stand me in good stead with the judge.

The lock-changing incident marked the beginning of the end for Lisa and me. From that moment on, she avoided any form of interaction. She grew increasingly distant and it became blindingly obvious that she was going to leave me. One of the few times we communicated was during a blazing argument in the course of which she smacked me in the back of my head with a bottle of wine. It sounds bizarre but at the time I thought it was funny, as it was such an over-the-top thing to do.

I should have taken her attitude as a sign that I needed to change my ways but I was too busy getting high. I was incredibly selfish for most of the time that I was with her. I even sold the microwave for drug money, which was probably the reason that she eventually upped and left. 'I bought it so I'm going to weigh it in for whiz,' I told her. 'It's your own fault for not giving me any money for my drugs.'

A couple of weeks later, Lisa moved into another flat in India House, at the opposite end of the building. She didn't storm out. She just quietly got her stuff together and left. She carried on letting me see Stephen though, which was probably the only thing that prevented me from going off on one.

'Whatever happens between us, please don't take my son away from me,' I told her, just before she left. 'That's the one thing you could do to me that would completely destroy me.'

Soon after she moved out, Lisa started going out with some Icelandic fella. I can remember thinking: 'What the hell does she want to get herself involved with somebody from Iceland for? They're a load of seal-fucking inbreds with six toes on each foot.' I wanted to smash the geezer's face in. As far as I was concerned, he was just some twatty Eskimo who lived in an igloo and hunted penguins for his tea. He was a geology student as well, he studied rocks. Can you get any more boring than that?

I really did want to kill the fucker but, looking back, I didn't even know him so I'm glad I didn't. He could have been an all right bloke for all I knew and I'd only got myself to blame for Lisa going off with him. If I hadn't have fucked things up she probably wouldn't have given him a second thought.

Now that there was zero chance we were going to get back together, I decided to go to court to try and establish visiting rights for Stephen. Lisa didn't always answer her door when I went round to see him and I wanted to make sure that I was able to spend the day with him as often as I could. It was a precautionary measure. I didn't want the Eskimo playing daddy to my son.

The court authorities were pathetic. They claimed they couldn't get hold of Lisa to issue her with a summons, even though she was living in the same block of flats. They even hired a private investigator to find her was but the supposed private eye was just as clueless as they were. It was frustrating, because I knew where she was but I couldn't tell them the truth, as she was going on regular trips to Iceland and I was worried that the council might decide to cut her housing benefits off. There was a chance that they would try and claim that she was no longer a permanent UK resident and I was concerned that she could end up with less money to spend on Stephen if they started asking questions.

As it happened, I needn't have bothered trying to make sure that Lisa couldn't legally stop me from seeing Stephen because she permanently fucked off to Iceland with him at the earliest opportunity.

'They're living over there for good now,' her mother casually informed me. 'She says that she's starting her life afresh with that new fella of hers.'

Nah, I thought, Lisa wouldn't do that to me. Stephen was the one thing in my life that meant more to me than the drugs. She wouldn't take him away from me like that, she just wouldn't. Or would she? What other choice did she have? She must have known that the only way I would leave her alone was if she went abroad.

To say that I was devastated would have been an understatement and to say that I was sorry would have been akin to saying that Princess Diana regretted that she hadn't worn her seatbelt. Stephen was out of my life and I had nobody to blame but myself. Every day I spent without him was a day of his life that I was never going to get to experience. I had thrown away the perfect family for a couple of bags of whiz. I'd sold my soul for a syringe and a yellowy-white paste that drained me of my health and emptied out my wallet.

As the weeks went by, I sunk deeper into despair. I holed myself up in my room and wouldn't talk to anyone. The only time I ever went out was to buy one of the two things that kept me going: drugs or food. All the happy memories I had of Stephen danced around in my brain, reminding me of what a special little boy I'd lost. I was living in squalor. My kitchen was a dump, full of bulging black bin bags, strewn around the floor. I was severely neglecting myself and despite everything that had happened, I was still hammering amphetamines twenty-four hours a day.

Ever since I was a teenager, I thought that life would be worth living when I had a son of my own. I could show the world that I was a dutiful father. Now that Stephen was growing up in Iceland, I felt I had failed in my duty as a parent and I was gutted that Lisa had relocated to a foreign country to get away from me. She had always been non-judgemental of me and I was convinced I'd lost the only person who would accept me for what I really was.

I'd fucked up everything.

During the period of deep depression that followed the loss of my son, I allowed a female friend to stay with me for a while to help take my mind off things. She was going through a rough patch as well. Her fella was in jail and she was having a rotten time of it.[35] I'm not going to lie. I was secretly hoping that I'd become romantically involved with her but she was adamant that she didn't want to do anything that might compromise our friendship.

'If you want a girlfriend I can find you one though. I don't want to complicate things by going there with you but I know a girl called Louise. I reckon you'd get on well with her.'

I wasn't sure if I was ready for another girlfriend. I was still missing Lisa and I was beginning to think that the female gender was some-how genetically predisposed to fuck me over. I had never got on with Mam, Thea had continued to dog me even after she was dead and the love of my life had taken my son and fucked off to a foreign country.

'Okay I'll meet her,' I grudgingly told my friend, 'but she better be a girl who will accept me for who I am. I can't be doing with someone who's going to be shocked by some of the things I've done in the past.' What I really meant to say was, 'This girl better be on my level because the mother of my child was a special woman.'

And as it turns out, Louise exceeded my wildest expectations. It was love at first sight and, every time I see her, I'm reminded of what a lucky man I am. The first time me and Lou met up, I thought 'wow!' She had an incredible depth to her. It was like I could see her soul staring back at me every time I looked her in the eyes. We'd had similar life experiences. She had a tough time with her mother and was later taken into care and she's had to fight tooth and claw for everything she's ever had. We were destined to be with one another.

Lou was living in Hyde, near Manchester, only a five-minute journey from me. The only obstacle that stood between us was one of her ex

---

[35] She's having a bit of a difficult time of it at the moment as well. Her and her fella were recently involved in a violent altercation, which resulted in her getting done for hitting somebody over the head with a shovel and him getting ten years for wounding with intent. She doesn't have the best of luck!

boyfriends. He was former armed forces and he fancied himself as a bit of a hard man. I'll refer to him as 'Chris'.

'Chris' had a naughty reputation and he'd managed to scare Louise's other recent boyfriends half to death. He was determined to control Lou's life even though they were no longer an item. The difference between me and her other boyfriends was that I didn't give a fuck, not because I was Superman but because I was used to dealing with the threat of violence. I'm not an easy person to intimidate and I had more important things to worry about than some plastic gangster trying to throw his weight around.

Soon after me and Louise had got together properly, Chris started phoning, talking shit. He even invited me round to see him, no doubt hoping that he could put on the frighteners and break Lou and me up. That might have worried some people but I didn't turn a hair.

'I'll get my coat. The fella's inviting me around to see his gaff,' I said.

Chris's face turned a pale shade of white when he saw me walking towards his door with Lou. He may have driven her previous boyfriends away but he sure as fuck couldn't bully me.

'How's it going, Chris?' I asked, pretending that I was oblivious to his feeble attempts to scare me. He looked fucking wounded.

'Yeah, not bad.'

He's six-foot tall and I'm small as fuck but he was afraid to lay a finger on me. What a fucking coward. After that, the silly bastard kept ringing Louise up, telling her that 'no-one's even heard of Benny'. Well it's not as if I was Al Capone. I was living in the real world, not the Mafioso fantasy land that he inhabited.

The next time Chris the so-called hard man rang our house, he was asking Louise to fill him in on what I thought of him, expecting her to tell him that I'd heard all about his gangster credentials and that I thought that he was the north-west's very own Tony Soprano.

'He thinks that you're a closet poof,' she told him.

Well she could hardly tell him a lie just to spare his feelings, could she? He definitely wasn't the gangland-enforcer type he tried to make himself out to be. He was a fucking joker but he had the gift of the gab and he was willing to do whatever it took to retain his grip on Lou.

Fearing that he would gradually lose his power over Louise, Chris even tried to drop me in it with the authorities.

'She's a drug addict and her boyfriend's selling speed,' he told them.

He was wrong. I wasn't selling drugs at that point but he was engaging in a variety of illegal activities. He was running the local working girls around the city, effectively acting as their pimp. Given that he was a well-known criminal, it was hypocritical of him to report me for failing to live within the law. He is one of those smarmy people who can worm their way round the authorities and convince them of anything. He had no real evidence that I was dealing drugs. Fair enough, he knew I was a user but I wasn't selling any on.

In a cruel twist of fate, Louise fell pregnant shortly after Chris grassed us up, meaning that the social services were hanging around her in the months leading up to the birth of our daughter. The fear of losing her child was the final straw for Lou and she started disappearing for weeks on end, calling in at various different hospitals up and down the country to get them to check that her baby was still okay. Ironically, the very people who had caused her to go insane with worry were about to use her fragile mental state as an excuse to put our daughter into care when she was born. They had hounded Lou until she was no longer capable of functioning and now it was time for them to persecute her for caring about the fate of her unborn child.

The minute that little Lily was born, the authorities were itching to take her away from us. It was a caesarean birth, which was weird because it meant I never got to see her coming out. As it turned out, holding her in my arms for the first time was the only major event I would get to share with her. The social services claimed that Louise wasn't in a fit state to look after her and our newborn baby was placed in a care home shortly after being brought into the world.

'The mother's suffering from schizophrenia,' the social workers told the child-protection service.

Well let's put it this way: she was perfectly all right until they threatened to snatch her unborn daughter.

'We think that she might have an alcohol problem as well. She's been seen with a bottle of wine outside the doctor's surgery.'

She'd taken a bag full of shopping with her to a mental-health appointment and it had a single bottle of wine in it, along with a dozen other items of food and drink. It was hardly enough to qualify her as an alcoholic. That's like saying that you're a gambling addict if you've played the lottery.

We would have got our daughter back if it wasn't for the surprise appearance of one Louise's estranged relatives, who I shall refer to as 'Pete'. He got to hear about the situation through either Lou's mam or her Auntie Carol and he made a play, through official channels, to get custody of Lily. It was ironic because Lou had only ever met him once. He hadn't taken much interest in her before so why was he so interested in adopting her child? If it was a choice between putting Lily up for adoption or allowing me to look after her then the authorities would almost certainly have chosen me. However, Pete had always stayed on the right side of the law, which made him a better parent for our baby in the eyes of the social services. But in my eyes he's a snide bastard and I'll never forgive him for what he did to me and Louise.

Pete looks like one of the Scousers in those Harry Enfield sketches and he's one of those overly friendly people who always try too hard. He comes across to me as a posh plastic Scouser from the Wirral and he's also a proper straight goer, which apparently means that he can raise my daughter better than her biological father can. Well let me tell you this: karma's a bitch and he's going to come unstuck big time.[36] You take someone's kid – even if it's done legally – and you're depriving them of something irreplaceable.

So there you have it. I thought I'd got off lightly after Operation Omega but, in reality, being banned from the football has destroyed my life in every conceivable way. The vacuum created by the lack of violence has plunged me into an endless spiral of drugs, depression and regret. I'd like to tell you that my story has a happy ending to it but it doesn't. I'm still taking the drugs (although I mostly tend to stick to the Dexedrine nowadays), Lisa and Stephen are still living overseas (although

---

[36] I'd like to make it clear that this isn't me issuing a threat towards him. All I'm saying is that, if there's any justice in the world, something bad will happen to him. I'm not saying that I would ever try to take my revenge on him because I am pretty sure he would go straight to the Old Bill.

I recently met up with my son while he was back in Manchester and there's a chance I'll get to see him again) and Pete the Scouser is still raising my daughter as his own.

Words can't begin to describe the pain of losing your children. I think about them every day. I miss them so much. Lily and Stephen, if you're reading this, I know I've made a lot of mistakes but I would never have given you up without a fight. If I could turn the clock back and live my life again would I go to the football? Yeah, probably. Would I do the drugs? Would I fuck. I'm not going to sit here and lecture you on the dangers of taking amphetamines but before you even consider whacking a needle in your arm, think about the consequences. I lost Lily through no fault of my own but I will never forgive myself for driving Lisa and Stephen away.

I acted selfishly and for that I am truly sorry.

26

THE GUVNORS TODAY

So what are my final thoughts on the Guvnors? This is the point of the book where the author usually attempts to spin the readers a yarn about how they're a changed man and how they've given up their life of violence to become a monk, well not me. I'm no longer an active football hooligan but I will always look back on the time that we spent together as an exciting and worthwhile part of my life. Lads like Frankie, Chrissie and Rodney were the nearest thing I had to a family and hooliganism elevated me from a nobody to a somebody. I'm not going to sit here and condemn the activity that has helped me to get through the traumatic experiences that have characterized my existence. I wouldn't encourage other people to do what I've done but it was what I needed to do to survive.

Much as I enjoyed going to the matches with the Guvnors, my years as a hooligan are nothing more than fading memories from a bygone era. I'm too old to be getting nicked for trumped-up charges and, more importantly, football violence isn't what it used to be. The days of three hundred-odd game lads scrapping in the street are long gone. You still get naughty little thirty-on-thirty fights but advances in technology have put an end to mass brawls. Nowadays there are wall-to-wall cameras at every ground and the dibble will arrest you for dropping a Mars Bar wrapper. Then there's the whole commercialisation issue. The likes of Danny Dyer and Dougie Brimson have transformed hooliganism into a multi-million-pound industry. It's a marketing trend and brands like Burberry and Paul and Shark are making money from people who like the image but would be the first to run in a brawl.

In all honesty, I probably look at the Young Guvnors era through rose-tinted glasses because it was such an exciting time to be alive. For me, the Seventies and Eighties will be the decades to remember. That said, for the current generation, hooliganism is very much alive and kicking. I see football violence as similar to punk. It's not like it was in its heyday but it's still around and it's changed and progressed over the years. This book wouldn't be complete without a contribution from a modern-day City hooligan and so I've decided to finish off with an account of the contemporary scene from some of our younger lads. They've requested that I leave their version of events unedited so here's what they've got to say.

It's nice to be able to tell people about the current scene at Man City. Just like at every other club, there are youth mobs and the older lads are still turning out, looking for a bit of aggro as well, no matter what the press might try and make you believe. One thing that the younger lads are gutted about is never being around for Maine Road. What a ground! The amount of stories we hear about the battles there amazes us. Still, I suppose if we'd never moved grounds then we would never have had all this investment in the club.

Anyways, one of my pet hates is the way that the public class us as scum and want to throw the book at us. It's not like we're out mugging, murdering people or any other disgusting habit that the proper scum of the earth seem to do. We're fighting with lads who want to do the same. It's sad that the police use all their funding up on stopping us when they could be putting it to better use. In a way it does hurt when you're slagged off by your own parents and they're constantly disappointed in you, but fuck it.

The following stories are by two of the lads who go with City's youth firms these days. I'll call them 'Mr C' and 'Mr T' (not the lad from the 'A-Team').

Stockport
We've had battles with a fair few mobs over the year and one of the teams we've had it with a few times is Stockport County, or as people like to call them, 'The Friendly Mob'. The first clash that we had with Stockport was back

when Millwall were playing Altrincham in the FA Cup. There were thirty-odd of the older firm in the pub opposite Tesco and City had a right mob with them that day. There were over a hundred out for the Cockneys but unfortunately City's Old Bill had wind of it and they were all out as well.

It got to the end of the game and around sixteen of us young lads wanted to go and look for the Cockneys. We started bouncing around looking for them, which led to one of our older Youth lads saying that we were mad. It's not the first time that's been said about us either!

We couldn't find Millwall and we later found out that they'd disap-peared sharpish after finding out what City had out. Fair enough there were only two minibuses full of them but still. Meanwhile, Stockport had been giving it the mouth, saying that they would be showing up. They were playing Staines.

We were being followed by the Old Bill all over Altrincham with cameras right in our faces, the lot. I used to work down there so I knew where to escape from the plod and we ran down to Dane Road away from them. Some lads had decided to give it a miss so thirteen of us got the train in the end. We were all off our rockers, sniffing all sorts of drugs. Some of us even had poppers.

After about twenty minutes, we arrived at Stockport train station and we were all bouncing to fuck. We found their pub and one of the lads walked in saying, 'Come on, we're here.'

County were confused and some of them ran inside the pub. At this time, we realised that we should have just smashed the pub up while we had the chance.

We made a move to Hollywood Park and then we stood at the top end, waiting for them. Then, instead of waiting for them to come to us, we decided to run headlong into them. The first lad into the fray started throwing digs but he missed with a few of them and he got tripped up by the Stockport lot. They started booting him in his head but he was laughing his head off the whole time.

A City lad jumped in and knocked a few Stockport lads out of the way but, in doing so, he did some damage to the lad on the floor. Now it was going off proper. Lads were fighting like fuck and some of the County mob were stood in the background watching. People were coming out of their homes, wondering what the hell was going on. A lad who was on the floor got up and almost got hit by one of his own lads in the confusion. Lads were being smashed to fuck over car bonnets, rammed into car doors, the lot.

Eventually the County lads disappeared and some of them even came up to shake our hands. One of the funniest moments in my life was when one of the County lads came up to us to ask us to give him back his shoe! Everyone was laughing, even Stockport were chuckling at it all and we eventually gave them the trainer back. Still, to this day, we don't know who robbed it.

Bolton

Where to start with them? From reading hooligan books and hearing stories from older lads from various clubs, they seem to have had a right good mob back in the yesteryear of football hooliganism, although there aren't many teams that rate them nowadays, especially with the current youth generation they have with them. Basically, they've never shown up in Manchester and the two times that I can remember when they actually did show their faces, one time they didn't even make it out of Victoria station, and the other, they got smashed to pieces outside a city-centre pub. Saying that though, credit where it's due. They're one of the few mobs that have ever gone into that pub.

We've had two clashes with Bolton and the first was in Darwen. We had been arranging it for a while and one of the lads had got the number of one of Bolton's lads a few weeks previously at a local match between two north-west teams. On the day of the game, eleven of us showed up at the agreed meeting point. It was annoying because some lads went to Bolton town centre and others just didn't turn up in the end.

After a few beers in Manchester, we gave Bolton a call and after a couple of minutes of them saying go here, there and everywhere, we gave up and decided to go into Oldham instead. Oldham were playing Millwall and we fooled around round there for a while and generally had a laugh.

After a few hours, we decided to make a move back into Manchester. We got in contact with Bolton and they told us that they'd been to Blackburn to see if Wigan or Blackburn were out. Ten of us made our way to Darwen, which was where Bolton said that they would be, and we were inside the pub for around ten minutes when some casually dressed lads started coming in. The lads that had just walked in claimed to be Wigan and some of us started chatting to them.

All of a sudden, there were objects being thrown at the doorway and some blokes were getting slapped. It was Bolton and they were having a go at some of the Wigan fans near the door. We ran round to confront them and then they steamed in. A lot of us were still in our teens and to see a load of fully grown blokes running at us was a weird sight, as we thought we'd arranged a fight with lads our own age. We later found out that it was their older youth along with some of the lads at Bolton who we actually rate.

In the end, the pub got smashed up and lads got bottles round their heads, pool cues on them; the lot. The only way they could get out of the room was through the main window of the pub. We gave as good as we got but we were eventually overpowered by large numbers.

After a while, the lads managed to get away due to the sirens being heard in the distance. The Wigan lads had stuck around and watched the whole thing happen and some twelve months later, one of them ended up in the shit thanks to some DNA found in the chewing gum he had dropped.

We tried flagging down taxis to get away but it was to no avail. We were eventually found by the police and eight of us were set for a night in the cells. Two lads were already in hospital so they luckily never had to visit the police station. Some of the Bolton lads were caught as well and, over the following day, lads were let out at various times on bail.

The next time we played Bolton, we were at their place the following season and nobody was out for it so we waited until the return game the same season to see if they finally turned up in Manchester. For whatever reason, the whole event was a fuck up, no thanks to the police in Bolton. There was no chance of revenge that day so it was left until the 2009/2010 season when, after a few years of going and not being done in at all, we had Bolton away.

We knew that this game would be police overkill and so we tried to stay away from Bolton town centre. We had a good-size older firm who went down and didn't encounter any problems, apart from Bolton telling them to travel miles out of the way for them. We ended up getting a bus to Bury to sneak into Bolton to meet them.

We were followed by the police all the way there and when we arrived in Bury, we had the local Football Intelligence Unit waiting for us. After being Section 60'd[37], we eventually made our way to the pub, where some

---

[37] Section 60 is a piece of police legislation referring to their powers of stop and search.

City and a few Bury had already settled down for a few beers. We were hoping that we'd bump into Bolton but the local police didn't leave our side all day and even our attempts to try and sneak out and all go in different pubs didn't manage to shake them.

Eventually it started getting dark and City's Football Intelligence Unit turned up. As we attempted to leave, we saw some Bolton in the area and they started getting mouthy, giving idle threats about what they'd do to certain people.

We ended up getting escorted onto the Metrolink and surprisingly, no police came on with us so we jumped off in Radcliffe, settled in another pub and then told Bolton where we were.

Shortly afterwards, one of the lads received a call so we all left the pub and went to where Bolton's mob were. A couple of Bury lads showed up for a nosey as well and came with us. We ran into Bolton down a passageway and we let out a chant of 'Youth! Youth! Youth!' and they started to back off.

More of Bolton's lads started getting out of cars and taxis, which led to a stand-off for a second. We then got back into them again and started to back them off. One of them got punched to the floor and got a kicking for his troubles. We've all done it! One of the lads ended up picking him up off the floor whilst his chums from Bolton were stood there watching what was happening. As all of this was going on, Bolton came back up, armed with bricks and bottles. A stick was smashed into one of the lads' faces and blood oozed out everywhere.

The tide then turned and Bolton started to back us up the alleyway and get the upper hand. It ended up with all of our lads getting on their toes, leaving four or five lads to have it with their lads. One lad got battered to fuck. He'd decided to stick it out and he got a kicking for it.

A lot of Bolton's firm had been inactive for the whole fight but now that there was an injured lad about, who was easy pickings, they started booting and punching him and taking pictures of it on a mobile phone. A certain lad also called for him to be stabbed. He knows who he is. Fortunately, one of his mates called for him to leave it out.

Eventually the police sirens started going and people decided to scarper. Little groups were chasing each other but the damage was already done.

Since then, Bolton have failed to turn up either at our place or for pre-arranged meets, even in their own backyard. Their older lads we have some respect for, just not this current young generation that they have. Every mob gets done and we're no different. It's just a shame that the two times we got done, it was by the same team.

Well there you have it: Mr C and Mr T seem to be having just as much fun as we did. It would be wrong for me to pin hooliganism down to one generation, just as it would be wrong for me to claim that we were the only firm worth speaking of in our day. Whether you support Oxford United or Accrington Stanley, every club has got a handful of proper lads associated with it and it's the passion that exists within each individual that keeps the scene alive. Football has had an impressive longevity: City have been around for a hundred years and in that time buildings have crumbled, nations have come and gone and countless people have lost their lives. Our team has survived because it has taken fans through the full range of emotions. Hooligans are the physical embodiment of those feelings, that's why football violence is such an enduring subculture and that's why our firm is still going strong, with a good two hundred members at its disposal.

Well I've set my life out and, now that you know me, I hope you will be able to look at hooligans from a different perspective the next time you see us being slagged off in the media. We're not the scum of the earth. We're normal people, bound together by our love of fighting. From Young Guvnor to not so young Guvnor, football has stayed with me throughout my life and, who knows, maybe there will be a sequel to this book. Until then, thank you for reading it and all the best.

GLOSSARY

AC	attendance centre
Beer monster	an older hooligan who likes to drink a lot
Bally	balaclava
Blag	robbery
Boat	face, as in boat race
Boozer	pub
Bottle	£2, as in a £2 bottle of glue
Brief	either a ticket or a solicitor
BTP	British Transport Police
Bubbler	an informant
Bubbling	giving information to the police
Carpet	£3
Carpet O	£30
Chiv	knife
Claret	blood
CSO	community service order
DC	detention centre
Deps	depositions
Dexies	Dexedrine tablets, a substitute for amphetamines
Dibble	police
Double carpet	£3
Dresser	somebody who dresses in terrace fashions
Faces	lads
FIO	football intelligence officer
Firm/mob	gang
Five-O	police (as in *Hawaii Five-O*)
Game	up for a fight
Gear	heroin
Gooner	an Arsenal fan
Got done	been beaten
Grafting	earning money though illegal means

Handy	hard
Hommes purple/ window panes	LSD
Hooky	knocked off
Hoolivan	a riot van with a CCTV camera on top, designed for dealing with hooligans
Hot	dodgy
JC	judge and chambers
Jib	avoid paying
Laid on	given on tick
Lad	a hooligan
Little fellas	ecstasy
LOMBARD	an acronym for 'Loads of Money But A Right Dickhead'
Manor	area
Make a raise	earn some money, usually through crime
Mars Bar	scar
Mickey	Scouser (Mickey Mouse = Scouse)
Midnight	overnight train to London, although it actually left at 12:25 a.m.
Milk train	slow train
Millwall brick	a cosh made out of tightly rolled newspaper
Moody	menacing
Moo moo	an idiot
Mugged off	disrespected
Munich	a Man United supporter. It's a reference to the Munich air disaster in 1958 in which eight of their players were killed. Some of our fans would wind them up by singing songs about what happened. I'm not saying that I agree with it but it's a word that has entered my vocabulary over the years, for better or for worse.[38]

---

[38] You can criticise us all you like for referring to United's lads as 'Munichs' but they use the phrase themselves. They even had a firm called 'The Young Munichs'.

Naughty	extreme or dangerous
Old Bill	police
On one	on drugs
On your toes	running away
On the tap	begging
Operation Omega	the name that the police used for their operation against us[39]
Phet	amphetamine
Plácido	£10, as in the opera tenor Plácido Domingo
PNC	police national computer
Potted	hit with a glass
QE2	Liverpool Crown Court
Rattler	train
RIC	remanded in custody
Rick	mistake
Row	fight
Rum	prone to breaking the law
Section 18	grievous bodily harm
Section 27	an act enabling the police to ban you from an area for up to forty-eight hours
Section 60	stop and search
Screw	prison guard
Script	prescription
Scarfer/shirter/ shirt wearer	a football fan who isn't involved in hooliganism
Shooter	gun
Snide	fake
Speeding	on speed
SPG	special police group
Straight goer/ straight member	law-abiding citizen
Stripe	slash mark

---

[39] Twenty-six lads got arrested during Operation Omega. Everyone apart from me and Paul Halliday was given a code name based upon a letter of the Greek alphabet. I was known simply as 'Bennion'.

Swag	merchandise sold outside concert venues or football stadiums
Swag workers	people who sell swag (see above)
TAG	Tactical Aid Group, another term for riot police
Taking liberties	taking the piss
Ted	dickhead
Tools	weapons
Weighed in	beaten up
Whiz	speed
Working the in-out	selling swag or tickets before or after a concert
Yid	a self-deprecating name adopted by the Tottenham supporters, paying homage to their roots as a team with a large Jewish following

ACKNOWLEDGEMENTS

Special thanks to Geoff Ollier, who always pointed the way in my darkest hours. Lisa, I'm sorry and to Louise, you know I'm always there for you. I think it's a shame your family aren't. Finally, I'd like to give a mention to my son Stephen and my daughter Lily so that they may know me.

I've also got to give a mention to Rodney, Carl, Crawford, Scooby, Stimo, Steph, Maynard, Mark, Big Spinner, Goddard, Duffy, Splodge, Smiler, Fitzy, Ossie, Shady Ady, Chris Beswick, Steve Hallows, Big Dave, Titch, Andy, Geordie, Tick Tack, Clitheroe, Bradford Delly, that sneaky Scouser Lancaster J, Eggy, Paulsy, Travis, Nick, Sean, Scott, Bootsy, Les Tate, Scotty, Pat B, Tony Walker, Alex, the Francis brothers, Martin T, all of the old Gorton The Business gang (Tommy Reilly, James Veale, Johnny Rynn, Craig Richards, Bushy, etc), the Levy Baseball Boys (Lee Tate, Howsey, Paul, Trevor F, etc), the Oldham lads, the Wythenshawe lads (Crossy, Little Dennis, etc), the Levenshulme lads, the Chesterfield lads, the Openshawe lads, the Moston lads, the Blackley lads, the Sale lads, the Hyde lads, the Bury lads and last but not least Noel Gallagher who used to come with us to every away game when City first went down.

Nemo me impune lacessit.

If anybody wants to get in touch with me about anything that has appeared in this book, my email address is:
andben0543@yahoo.co.uk